Zell Miller

MODERN AMERICAN STATESMAN SERIES
★ ★ ★

A Senator Speaks Out on
Patriotism, Values *and* Character

MONUMENT
PRESS

Zell Miller:
A Senator Speaks Out On Patriotism, Values, and Character
by Monument Press

Printed in the United States of America

ISBN 0-9769668-2-4

601 Pennsylvania Avenue, N.W.
Suite 900, South Building
Washington D.C., 20004
202-220-3195

www.MonumentPress.com

A NOTE FROM THE PUBLISHER

Monument Press is proud to present the *Modern American Statesmen Series*. This series offers the best in public speeches and remarks given by our most prominent elected officials. All the material in the series was originally spoken from the floors of the U.S. House of Representatives and the U.S. Senate.

Throughout American history, members of Congress have given important speeches and remarks from the floors of the House and Senate. From Senator Thomas Jefferson's floor discourses on Federalism to Senator John F. Kennedy's floor speeches on Civil Rights to Senator Richard Nixon's floor lectures on communism, they constituted the fundamental nature of public opinion and public discourse of their time.

Today, during hearings, debates, and floor proceedings, members of Congress still weigh issues of monumental national importance. We believe their words should be published and distributed in a manner that is accessible to the general public. The material herein gives the reader the best thoughts of United States senators and representatives. It sheds light on the past, present, and future of the nation's laws and policies, covering issues of war and peace, taxation, education, national security, general welfare, health and social security, morality, and others.

The speeches in this book will be found authentic and accurate. They are published as spoken and recorded by Congress. As such, some of the grammar, syntax, and sentence structure may not conform to normal editorial styles. The words are published just as they were spoken.

The *Modern American Statesmen Series* is a non-partisan project. We aim to give the reader the mere truth about what's been spoken on the floors of the House and Senate, with no commentary or observation.

The series is compiled and edited by Bryan T. Mullican, Senior Editor of Monument Press. An editor, researcher and award-winning journalist, Mullican previously served as a Research Analyst for the Republican National Committee during the 2004 Presidential Campaign and also as Managing Editor of *The Tower* newspaper at The Catholic University of America.

Thomas M. Freiling
Publisher, Monument Press
Washington, D.C.

TABLE OF CONTENTS

" No one in America should have to work more than four months out of a year to pay the IRS, and in peacetime, the federal government should never take more than 33% out of anyone's pay check. "

TAX CUTS

January 22, 2001

Mr. President, I am very pleased to join with Senator Gramm as a sponsor of this important piece of legislation, first because it is an opportunity to reach across party lines and really practice bipartisanship, not just talk about it. But I'm even more pleased to be a cosponsor because of the far-reaching consequences of this bill.

Right now, our taxes have never been higher. Right now, our surplus has never been greater. To me, it's just common sense you deal with the first by using the second.

Remember that old Elvis Presley song, "Return to Sender." Well, that's what we want to do with this overpayment of taxes.

As some of you know, I've been in politics for a long time, and I thought I had seen it all. But when I came to Washington last year I was not prepared for the shock of just how matter of factly Congress ate into the surplus, gobbled it up indiscriminately and without hesitation on both sides of the aisle.

I couldn't believe it and it became clear to me that if we don't send this overpayment of taxes back to those who paid it, much of it will be frittered away, and I think most Americans have enjoyed as much of that as they can stand.

Some of my colleagues talk of "targeted" tax cuts, and I respect their opinion, I respect them. But here's how I think about that: who are we to pick and choose and cull and select and single out among our taxpayers.

Who are we to play "eeny, meany, miney, mo," with them. All of them combined have paid more than it takes to run this government. And all of them combined should get a break from this oppressive tax structure of ours.

This plan would make our tax code more progressive by cutting federal income taxes for people all across the income spectrum, and the largest percentage cuts would go to those Americans who earn the least. Under this proposal, six million families will no longer pay any federal income taxes at all. That's one out of five families with children.

Any time I look at a tax cut, I always apply it to the family I grew up in: a single parent with two children. Under the current rate, that single parent begins paying taxes when she earns $21,300. Under this plan, she would not become a taxpayer until her earnings reach $31,300.

Lower taxes gives Americans a better chance at a better standard of living. It can mean the difference between renting or buying a home. Today, it can be the difference between being able, or not being able, to pay your heating bill.

No one in America should have to work more than four months out of a year to pay the IRS, and in peacetime, the federal government should never take more than 33% out of anyone's pay check.

I also believe this tax cut could help provide some needed insurance against a long-lasting economic slow down. But most importantly, and why I'm here, is that I agree with President Bush that the taxpayers are much better judges of how to spend their own money than we are.

When I was governor of Georgia, I was proud that in my state we cut taxes by more than a billion dollars. As a U.S. Senator, I'm looking forward to cutting taxes in this nation by more than a trillion dollars.

[Congressional Record: S312-313]

December 20, 2001

Madam President, I, too, will have a few remarks on the economic stimulus bill. I think a decision not to have a straight up-or-down vote on it and let the majority of this Senate prevail, regardless of the makeup of the majority, is a mistake. I know it is a loss for the country and the folks who need our help and need it immediately.

Why do we always have to act as if we are in a football game where one side, one team, has to win and the other team has to lose? Why can't we have both parties the winners, along with the American people?

Myself, when it gets down to the block, I am kind of a half-a-loaf man. Whether it is 75 percent, 65 percent, or 50 percent, when you get right down to it, that is always better than zero percent. You can eat half a loaf. Having no loaf at all may make a political point, but in the end somebody goes hungry.

This is not the House bill. I could never have supported that bill. I would never have voted for it. This compromise package does not include everything either side wanted. Instead, it represents a reasonable compromise.

Some say speeding up the reduction of the tax rates from 27 percent to 25 percent is just helping the wealthy. Nothing could be further from the truth. The folks who benefit from this are folks who earn as little as $27,000 a year, going up to $67,000 a year. For married couples, this rate reduction would help those who earn between $47,000 to $120,000 a year. Those are not the wealthy or the rich. Those are middle-income Americans. Many are our friends and organized labor. This bill also includes a $300 rebate for those who did not get anything from the earlier tax cut.

On the health insurance area, we recognize the need to help the unemployed by providing health insurance for them. This is a very significant change. This is a dramatic change and should be welcomed by both Republicans and Democrats alike.

Some argue that the best way to give laid-off workers access to health care is to provide a 75-percent subsidy for COBRA premiums, as well as access to State Medicaid Programs. Others disagreed and preferred a broader tax credit for health insurance premiums. This package falls somewhere in between, providing a 60-percent advanceable, refundable tax credit for all health insurance.

It is not a whole loaf for anyone, but it represents a practical solution, and it is the best way to do what we all want; that is, to help the workers and help them before it is too late.

The package also includes help for State governments, something our Governors and legislators desperately need right now. It provides almost $5 billion in payments to State Medicaid Programs. This does not represent everything States or many of us wanted. I was hoping to get a fix for the upper payment limit but, again, it is half a loaf.

As it is, we have no loaf. We have no loaf at all. We do not even have a slice. Who was it who said, Let them eat cake?

I yield the floor.

[Congressional Record: S13836-13837]

February 6, 2002

Mr. President, I hear today we are about to have a funeral, that the stimulus bill is on life support, and that the plug will be pulled sometime today. The cause of death? Partisan politics. It is a shame, although perhaps the money can now be applied to the deficit, which has concerned some of us, and we will be closer to a balanced budget.

The soon-to-be-deceased could have been saved. We had a reasonable compromise right before we adjourned for Christmas. The President supported it. Some Democrats, including this one, supported it. It had a majority of the votes in the Senate. Right now, if it had passed, it could have already been signed, the rebates could be being prepared, a reasonable health care benefit could have been a reality—such promise. Who was it who wrote that the saddest words of word or pen are that it might have been—something like that?

This week we could have made the tax cut permanent. We could have added a capital gains tax cut. That is what Senator Gramm and I have advocated for some time.

No one ever stated so well how powerful an effect a cut in the capital gains tax could have on the economy as a Democrat, President John F. Kennedy. I quote:

"The tax on capital gains directly affects investment decisions ... the mobility and flow of risk capital from static to more dynamic situations ... the ease or difficulty experienced by new ventures in obtaining capital ... and thereby the strength and potential for growth of the economy."

That was Jack Kennedy, not the *Washington Times* or the *Wall Street Journal* or Lawrence Kudlow or Phil Gramm or Bob Novak. That was John Kennedy, a Democrat.

Over the years, he was not the only member of my party who advocated cutting the capital gains tax as a good way to stimulate the economy. Senator Patrick Moynihan, that wise and brilliant former Member of this body, consistently advocated it over the years.

What history shows is that, once upon a time, Democrats were tax cutters. I wish I could bring that time back. I rise today to strongly advocate making the tax cut we passed last year permanent and to cut the capital gains tax rate.

Unfortunately, the tax cut we passed last year, although it was a great tax cut, was compromised on its way to final passage. What started out as a broad, immediate, and permanent tax cut became one where some of the tax relief is delayed by several years. Then to add insult to injury, the whole thing is to be repealed in 2010.

We do something that, to my knowledge, Congress never had the gall to do before on a broad basis. We sunset individual tax cuts. We have done that several times with business tax revisions. But to individuals, to families, we have never done it where we gave them their money back and then took it away again later. That is playing games with our taxpayers. We should never do that. Eliminate the uncertainty of this tax cut and you will stimulate our economy. How can anyone make any long-range plans for a business or for a family with a here-today, maybe-gone-tomorrow tax cut, a tax cut that has a perishable date on it like a quart of milk?

The fastest way to show taxpayers we are serious about tax relief—the only way, really—is to make the tax cut permanent. The fastest way to prompt businesses to expand and to invest is to cut the capital gains rate from 20 to 15 percent. We are not in a slump just because consumer sales are down. We are in a slump because venture capital fell 74 percent in the past year. Capital spending by businesses is at its lowest in decades.

As Senator Gramm said, every time we have cut the capital gains rate— every time—tax revenues have risen, not fallen, and asset values have always shot up.

Today a capital gains tax cut would bring even better results because today's stock market is no longer the playground of the rich. Almost half of all Americans now own stock, and almost a third—one out of three—who earn less than $30,000 a year own stock. Aren't those the people whom we Democrats say we want to help? The American middle class has become, for the first time in our history, the American investment class.

So as I eulogize this soon-to-be-deceased, I think of the bruised and battered Marlon Brando's *On The Waterfront*—what could have been. We could have had a contender.

[Congressional Record: S386]

June 3, 2004

Madam President, I rise today to join with my colleagues in celebrating this anniversary. In 2001 and again in 2003, Congress had the wisdom to pass two bold tax cut plans. I firmly believe they were the key to turning around this economy.

When the President came to office, the economy was already taking a turn for the worse. Job growth was slowing down, the stock markets were moving in the wrong direction. A dose of strong medicine was needed. Our President came up with a bold plan for tax relief, to get more money out of Washington and put it back into the pockets of workers and the small business owners who earned it.

President Bush knows, as President Kennedy knew, and as President Reagan knew, the best way to jump-start the economy is to leave more money in the hands of the American people.

When people and businesses can keep more of their own money in their own pockets instead of having to send it to the "National Center for Income Redistribution on the Potomac," it follows they will spend more and they will invest more and they will expand their businesses more. When that happens, the result is new jobs and a growing economy. That is exactly what has happened.

I was proud to be a cosponsor of those tax relief plans which lowered the tax bills for 111 million taxpayers, including 25 million small business owners. Americans have been using this extra money to pay their bills, get the kids in new clothes, or start a saving plans for themselves. Small businesses are investing in new equipment and expanding their operations. Workers are opening their 401(k) statements to see the numbers are going up instead of down.

As a result, our economy is on the upswing. We have had 10 consecutive quarters of economic growth. In the last 3 quarters, the economy has been stronger than any 3 consecutive quarters in nearly 20 years. Jobs are coming back, too. More than 1.1 million jobs have been created since last August and more are on the way. Manufacturing activity is picking up, and the business community is more confident than ever that they feel this turnaround taking root.

President Bush has done an outstanding job shepherding our economy through these tough times. I have one wish as we celebrate this anniversary. I wish this Congress would take one more step with these tax cuts. I wish we would do what we should have done in the first place, make these tax cuts permanent.

I have asked this question before and I will ask it again: How can anyone, how can any business, make any long-range plans for a business or for a family with a "here today, gone tomorrow" tax cut, a tax policy that has a perishable date on it, like a quart of milk?

The fastest way to show our taxpayers we are serious about tax relief, the fastest way to ensure this economic growth continues, is to make the tax cuts permanent.

I yield the floor.

[Congressional Record: S6390-6391]

" What can we do, and what can we do quickly, to stop this brain drain from our schools? How can we make teaching more competitive with better paying professionals? I will tell you how we could have an immediate effect. Let our teachers keep more of their hard-earned money. "

EDUCATION

April 17, 2002

Madam President, I am at heart a teacher. Perhaps it is genetic, for I am the son of teachers. Whatever its source, a commitment to education runs deep in my soul. That is why, when I was Governor of Georgia, I chose to focus on education, for all our other challenges have at their root the same solution: Children who are loved and children who are educated.

I believe education is everything. It is the educated individual who makes this Nation stronger. It is the educated individual who adds to its wealth, protects against enemies, carries forward its ideals and faith.

The Latin phrase "alma mater" means "nourishing mother." That is a pretty good description of what our schools should be for our children.

Within those schools, all education starts with the teacher standing at the head of the child's classroom. Teachers are the world's most noble creatures, engaged in the world's most noble profession. Teachers are the architects who guide and shape the building of young lives. Teachers are the ones who call forth the best from our children and inspire them to reach new heights. Teachers, I think we would all agree, are the key ingredient to improving education.

So if we are to build a first class education system in this country, we must be able to attract and hold on to good teachers. Right now, we are losing that battle. We are losing that fight badly.

Last year we set a new standard in Federal aid for education with the passage of President Bush's far-reaching education reform bill. But while we have made big strides in Federal funding for education, we still have not touched teacher salaries at the Federal level.

I would argue that teacher pay is the most important area of all education. Yet our teachers work in sometimes deplorable conditions and for little pay. Public school teachers in America today make an average of $43,335 a year. One would assume that about half of the States have teacher salaries above the national average and the other half have teacher salaries below that level. But actually, only 12 States, plus the District of Columbia, have salaries that are higher than the national average. The other 38 States are below the national average. In fact, the dollar gap between the lowest and the highest average salaries varies greatly from a low of $30,265 in South Dakota to a high of $53,281 in New Jersey.

Sadly, our teachers have even lost financial ground over the past few years. In the past decade, teacher salaries rose only one-half of 1 percent when inflation is taken into account. In many States, teachers actually lost ground to inflation.

Today in this Nation, teacher salaries account for a smaller proportion of total education spending than they did 40 years ago. In 1960, the average education expenditure devoted to teacher salaries was 51 percent. Today it is 36.7 percent, the lowest percentage since records have been kept.

As a result, many of the best and brightest of our young people today steer away from the classrooms to join the ranks of better paying professions. It has become clear that unless we in Congress take some drastic action, and take it soon, this disparity will only get worse because on the horizon ominous storm clouds loom darkly. We must hire 2 million more teachers in the next decade to keep up with new students who are entering our schools. Where are we going to get all those new teachers? Where?

Enrollment at our colleges of education is down 30 percent. Among those who are willing to try teaching, 40 percent leave the profession before the end of their fifth year. In some States, almost 20 percent leave after just 1 year. Most, of course, leave to pursue better paying careers. And who can blame them? It is a hollow message when we constantly tell our teachers how invaluable they are and then pay them so little.

What can we do, and what can we do quickly, to stop this brain drain from our schools? How can we make teaching more competitive with better paying professionals? I will tell you how we could have an immediate effect. Let our teachers keep more of their hard-earned money.

I will be introducing a bill to give our teachers an immediate pay raise in the form of a tax cut. Simply put, teachers would keep more money in their pocket each payday and send less of it to the IRS. They need this money back home more than we need it up here. And I guarantee you they will spend it more wisely than we will. Hard-earned money always goes further in a household than it does in a rat hole. I call it the Thank You Teachers Tax Cut. Here is how it would work.

It would include every full-time teacher, public and private, in every pre-kindergarten and K through 12 classroom. This tax cut would start immediately and would increase the longer the teacher stayed in the classroom.

Teachers with fewer than 5 years in the classroom, about 900,000 teachers, would get a tax cut equal to one-third of their Federal income tax. Teachers with 5 to 10 years of experience, also about 900,000 teachers, would get to keep two-thirds of what they would normally pay in Federal income tax. Teachers with more than 10 years' experience—about 1.8 million teachers—would have no Federal income tax at all for as long as they stayed in the classroom.

The Thank You Teachers Tax Cut would mean immediate pay raises of between 5 and 15 percent. It would put more money into teachers' pockets each and every payday. It would immediately give some equity to this noble profession. But it would be more than just more money. It would be a tangible show of our respect and our gratitude to this profession that is all too often taken for granted.

So it would be a huge tax cut, more than $16 billion a year at a minimum—probably more, according to my very rough math. But when we are talking about a projected budget for 2003 of $2.085 trillion, $16 billion is not even 1 percent of that budget. Don't tell me we cannot tighten our belt that little to help our teachers.

We all know our teachers are not paid adequately. They are not in my State and they are not in your State. Some need more help than others. Mississippi has the lowest average salary for teachers in the South and South Dakota has the lowest paid teachers in the Nation. I would plead for the leaders of both parties in this Senate to support this tax cut.

I also think our Nation's Governors would like this proposal for two reasons: First, it does not interfere with the States' rights to set teacher salaries. But it does boost the bottom line for every State's teachers, and that is what is important.

Our Governors will also like it because today, and especially in the next few years, that Pac-Man called Medicaid is going to gobble up State revenues as never before. I warn you, that will leave a much smaller pot of money available at the State level for teacher pay raises.

I realize there are shortages in other important professions that have low salaries and bad working conditions, and I have great sympathy for those workers, too. But the long-term security of this Nation is wrapped up in our schools, and that is why this tax cut for teachers is such an important one now.

This tax cut is a chance to really help our children by making sure we put good teachers in their classrooms and keep them there. It is also a chance to help our deserving teachers. It is the fastest, surest way to put more money into their pockets immediately.

Finally, this is a chance for the Senate, for the entire Congress, to say thank you to our teachers.

[Congressional Record: S2760-2761]

" The proper role of managed care is to balance

the cost of health care with the medical needs of

patients, but in too many cases the concerns about cost

always come out ahead of the concerns for the patient.

In far too many cases, managed care has

become mismanaged care. "

PATIENTS' BILL
OF RIGHTS

June 20, 2001

M r. President, I rise in support of the McCain-Edwards-Kennedy patient protection bill of which I am very proud to be a cosponsor.

It is time—it is past time—for us to help millions of Americans obtain their basic rights and protections in dealing with health care providers.

It is time—it is past time—for health insurers to be held accountable when they show more concern for their own bottom line than for the patients' health and safety.

It is time—it is past time—for medical decisions to be made by patients and doctors, not some HMO bean counter.

I am no stranger nor a Johnny-come-lately to this issue. Years ago I became a supporter of Congressman Charles Norwood's effort, my good friend and Republican colleague from Georgia, as he went about in his courageous effort to make this change. And I come from a State that passed a strong patient protection law 2 years ago which, by all accounts, is working very well.

Now it is time for Congress to pass a strong Federal law to protect the millions of patients who cannot be protected by the Georgia law or by any other State's law.

This patient protection issue has been on our to-do list for a long time. We often speak of something serious as being a life-or-death matter, but it seldom is. Today this is truly a life-or-death matter for many American families who cannot wait any longer for us to act.

When Georgia wrestled with this issue 2 years ago, at the heart of the debate was the question of how we could best protect the interest of patients enrolled in managed care plans. That question has become increasingly important over the past 20 years because managed care has come to dominate the health care delivery system.

In 1980, managed care was a novelty. Today more than 70 percent of Americans and close to 80 percent of insured employees are covered by some form of managed care.

As the number of Americans enrolled in HMOs and managed care has grown, so have the complaints grown and so have the horror stories grown about being denied adequate care.

The proper role of managed care is to balance the cost of health care with the medical needs of patients, but in too many cases the concerns about cost always come out ahead of the concerns for the patient. In far too many cases, managed care has become mismanaged care.

The Georgia law that was passed in 1999 brought balance to the equation by giving patients explicit access to specialists and emergency care. The law also created an independent external review system to address patients' grievances. These are the essential components of any good bill, and they are the components of the bill I speak for today.

When the Georgia Legislature debated this law, there were critics—critics who made the same arguments that we are hearing in Washington today and that I heard last year and the year before.

In Georgia, the critics paid for ads saying the law would drive up premiums and cause more people to lose coverage. The critics paid for ads claiming employers would be held liable for HMO mistakes. They paid for ads predicting—and I love this alliteration—a "flurry of frivolous" lawsuits. Oh, there was hissing and moaning, but you know what? None of those dire predictions has come true. By all accounts, Georgia's patient protection law is working, and working well. In fact, patients are so satisfied with the independent review process that not a single, solitary patient has filed a lawsuit. No, not one.

Let me read from an article in the Atlanta Constitution on Monday, "Georgia's Pioneer Plan Avoids Legal Side Effects." The first two paragraphs I will read:

When Georgia's Patient's Bill of Rights became law two years ago, managed-care companies predicted they would be spending a lot of time in court defending their decisions to deny coverage. But there has yet to be a lawsuit filed by a patient who first aired the grievance through the new independent review system, state officials said.

"The law is working as intended," said Clyde Reese, Director of the Health Planning Division that oversees the patient protection process. "In the two years, no one who has gone through this process and has been denied has filed a lawsuit. It has not given rise to litigation. We're not aware of even one suit that's been processed."

There it is. The naysayers, Chicken Littles, never give up. Today on this bill, they are telling you that if it is passed, the sky will fall. They claim that the patients' employers can be sued as well as the HMO itself.

Wrong. Not so. This conservative, pro-business, Democratic Senator would never support a bill that exposes employers to that kind of liability. The McCain-Edwards bill specifically protects employers, gives protection even to the directors of the HMO. Those individuals cannot be personally sued, as some would have you believe. Employers are shielded from lawsuits unless they directly participate in a medical treatment decision.

This is also one of the very principles President Bush has said must be included. When President Bush released his principles for a bipartisan Patients' Bill of Rights on February 7, he said: Only employers who retain responsibility for and make medical decisions should be subject to suit.

We agree with President Bush. The principle outlined in February is the exact principle that is in our bill.

Now I am not a judge, and there is not enough of me to be a jury, but that is pretty plain to me. Only the HMO itself can be sued. And who can argue that HMOs should not be held accountable for mistakes? Shouldn't HMOs be treated like any other health care organization or doctor or business or individual?

While the Georgia law is a model for protecting patients, they unfortunately cannot protect all of Georgia's patients. No State law on this issue can protect all the citizens because a Federal law, the Employee Retirement Income Security Act of 1974, also known as ERISA, exempts a large class of employees from State oversight. That means millions of Americans are not covered under any patient protection law. They have no legal recourse in dealing with their HMOs, and they are suffering. It is, for too many, truly a life-or-death matter. That is why I believe so strongly that Congress must act, and act now.

The McCain-Edwards bill would also provide patients with their basic rights and protections in a balanced way. It guarantees access to medical specialists; it protects patients from having to change doctors in the middle of treatment; it provides fair, unbiased, and timely internal and independent external review systems to address patients complaints; it ensures that patients and doctors can openly discuss all the treatment options without regard to costs; and it includes an enforcement mechanism that ensures these rights are real.

The McCain-Edwards bill is also consistent with all of the principles laid out by President Bush except one: President Bush, a man for whom I have profound respect, wants the Federal courts to have exclusive jurisdiction over patient protection lawsuits. Another bill introduced by Senators Breaux and Frist, colleagues for whom I also have great respect, would comply with the President's wish on this point by moving all liability lawsuits to the Federal courts.

I am sorry, but I must respectfully disagree with the President and my colleagues on this one point. A purely Federal solution is not the best solution. The Breaux-Frist bill would preempt Georgia's law, as well as the laws of seven other States that have passed similar patient rights bills. The traditional arena for resolving questions about medical negligence is the State court. I submit that is where the jurisdiction should remain. It is the courtroom that is the closest to the people. Don't make my folks in Brasstown Valley have to go over the mountains, through Unicoi Gap, to get to that big, crowded, white marble courthouse in faraway Gainesville. That "ain't" right. Let 'em go to the county seat, to the courthouse in Hiawassee that they and their family have known for years.

Now, one more thing. Any bill on this issue is going to add to the cost of health insurance premiums. They all do. Ours, in my opinion, is the most reasonable. The Congressional Budget Office estimates if the McCain-Edwards bill is passed, premiums will increase by 4.2 percent over 10 years.

That translates to slightly more than $1 a month for the average employee. I believe most Americans will be more than willing to pay an extra $1 a month for the protection this bill will afford them.

Let's not drag this thing on. Please, let's not play partisan games with something this important. It has been an issue in three congressional elections now and two Presidential elections. The time has come to resolve this.

[Congressional Record: S6488-6489]

"The elderly are waiting for something else, too. They are waiting for us to do something about their needs. So far, they have waited in vain, each day growing older and weaker and many dying. Do you know who we in Washington are like? We are like those people in the biblical story of the Good Samaritan who passed by the man in the ditch and refused to help him. We are no better than they are."

Medicare
Prescription Drugs

April 9, 2002

M
r. President, there is a little family restaurant in my hometown of Young Harris, GA, that is called Mary Ann's. It is where the locals gather, and often some tourists, to enjoy the north Georgia mountains. It is a good cross-section of folks: Blue-collar laborers who build houses and cut timber; teachers from the little junior college up the street where I once taught, and may do so again; young folks determined to eke out a living without having to move to Atlanta; retired folks who did go to the city to find work and then came back home as soon as they could.

There is also a percentage of people from States such as New York and Michigan who dreamed of retiring to the sunshine of Florida, and did. Some found it a little crowded and then came on up to our area in north Georgia. We call them halfbacks. They retired to Florida, then moved halfway back home. Nothing wrong with Florida, mind you. They just enjoy the beauty of our mountains.

The point I am making is this is a great cross-section of folks, usually equally divided between Republicans, Democrats, and Independents. It is where I do my focus groups, for free—or not exactly for free: sausage, a biscuit, and a cup of coffee.

I suggest to both parties in Washington who pay those enormous sums of money for focus groups and polling that there is a much cheaper way to do it, and I swear I believe it is just about as accurate.

Anyway, the point I want to make is over the recess I was in Mary Ann's a lot, and I processed a lot of information on the cross-tabs of my brain, you might say.

One day, an old timer, so thin he was mostly breath and britches, followed me out into the parking lot. That is where you can have real private conversations, usually with one leg propped up on the bumper of a pickup. We have known each other all of our lives. He stared deep into my eyes and he said: "Zell, I am worried about Hoyle."

Hoyle Bryson is my uncle, kind of like a father since my dad died when I was a baby. Hoyle has always lived next door. When I was a little boy, he played professional baseball in the minor leagues at far-away and exciting places such as Tallahassee, FL; Tarboro, NC; Portsmouth, VA. Most of his life he was a hunter and a trapper and worked as a lineman for the Rural Electric Association. He is 88 years old now, has lived alone for over 20 years since his wife died. Once, a strong mountain man, he now has diabetes, prostate cancer, recently had angioplasty, and this week was bothered with a kidney infection. That once strong body is gradually growing weaker.

So I am worried about Hoyle. I am worried about Hoyle, even though he still makes his own garden and keeps a passel of hound dogs, as he always has.

I took him to the doctor a few weeks ago and stopped back with him at the drugstore to fill his prescriptions. They came to well over $100 and will only last him a couple of weeks.

Hoyle, as do most of our elderly, lives below what statistically is known as the lower poverty level threshold. This is the group that is hurt most by taxes and especially by rising health care costs. They are a valuable human resource that we must be, as my mountain friend said, worried about. It is not always pleasant and uplifting to see this segment of our society. They make us sad. Many of us—too many—even refuse to see them. We refuse to see them because we fear we may see ourselves to be the lonely elderly waiting, waiting for someone, anyone, to knock on their screen door and, as John Prine sings, say, "Hello in there."

The elderly are waiting for something else, too. They are waiting for us to do something about their needs. So far, they have waited in vain, each day growing older and weaker and many dying.

Do you know who we in Washington are like? We are like those people in the biblical story of the Good Samaritan who passed by the man in the ditch and refused to help him. We are no better than they are.

Our elderly have always been the backbone of our society, and if we do not give them some help soon, this Nation is going to get a permanent curvature of the spine.

Twenty-five centuries ago, Plato said it best: "States are as men are. They grow out of the character of man"—and woman, I might add.

If we in the Senate are to be called civilized, decent, God-fearing and God-obeying, we who are so richly blessed must meet this stark question of human need. We must have a meaningful prescription drug benefit, and we must have it soon.

I say to my fellow Senators, let us get our priorities in order. Sure, it was important to pass campaign finance reform, to try to take big money out of the political process. But is there anyone who would argue it is more important than a prescription drug benefit?

Election reform, we are going to get back on that. I am for it, too. We need to make the process easier, and we need to make it fairer. Fast-track trade, let's debate it. It is important.

These important time-consuming, well-meaning pieces of legislation that will tie this body in knots and run out the clock, are any of them close to dealing with the clear human need of a prescription drug benefit for our elderly?

If someone tuned in to the debates in this Senate since Christmas, they would conclude we care more about the welfare reform of the caribou than we do about the welfare reform of our elderly. This is a life-and-death issue about our fellow human beings, for goodness' sake. It is not about the fragility of the tundra in some far away isolated place only a very few people will ever see. It is about the fragility of a human being's last days on Earth.

There is absolutely no reason, no reason except cheap political gamesmanship, that we can't have a prescription drug benefit before election day— no good reason, no acceptable reason at all.

There are 11 prescription drug bills pending in this Senate today, all of which would be better than what we have. With 54 different Senators listed as cosponsors, that says to me a majority of this Senate wants to do something and do it now. All of the budget proposals floating around out there include money for a prescription drug benefit.

Both parties made this promise to our elderly in the 2000 election. So why are we waiting? How much longer must we wait? How long are we going to continue to play this nonproductive, partisan, never ending ping-pong game of retribution and payback that takes up so much valuable time and, frankly, makes us all look silly and petty? How long will we keep using the antiquated rules that slow down everything to a crippled snail's pace, that on a regular basis thwarts the clear will of the majority of this body and instead substitutes the tyranny of a minority? We should stop this dilatory dillydallying and put up a sign around here that says "No Loitering."

We should cut down on some of this Presidential candidate posturing. I know you cannot do away with all of it, of course. But you want to be a contender? Quit preaching and preening and produce. You want the well off to show you the money? Show the not so well off a prescription drug benefit.

To do that, you will have to say no to some of those high-priced political strategists, those consultants who couldn't get elected dogcatcher themselves, whose advice is always the same: Have an issue, not a result. Never compromise, never accept a half of loaf of anything.

Remember FDR once said:

"Try something. If it doesn't work, try something else. But for God's sake, try something."

That is what I am trying to say. I want Hoyle and all those millions like him in the land of plenty who have played by the rules and worked hard all of their lives to have some peace and hope in the twilight days of their last years.

If this so-called center of democracy keeps piddling and procrastinating and postponing this issue, I hope the American people will rise up as did those fans at that football game in Cleveland and run both teams off the field.

[Congressional Record: S2383-2384]

May 23, 2002

Mr. President, I know the hour is late and the day has been long and the staff and the pages and the Presiding Officer are tired. And so is this Senator. But I would like to take about 7 or 8 minutes to talk about a subject that is very dear to my heart.

Mr. President, "Honor thy father and thy mother" is the fifth of God's holy commandments.

For many of us—especially at my age—we can no longer do that (except in memory). We had our chance, and now they are gone. I never knew my father, and my mother died in 1986 when she was 93.

For those of us who have lost parents, we will be forever burdened by the haunting question: Did we adequately fulfill that commandment or could we have done more?

And, if one has a heart instead of a stone, we look around and see other living mothers and fathers whom it is not too late to still honor. I know I do.

And that is why I rise again—as I will do ad nauseum until something is done—to plead for action on prescription drugs before the August recess.

We must attack this problem by addressing both sides of the equation—prescription drug coverage and prescription drug cost.

We cannot truly help our seniors unless we increase the coverage and lower the cost. Coverage and cost.

I am a cosponsor of three bills that would do both those things.

First, Senator Bob Graham of Florida and I have introduced a bill that would increase coverage by adding an affordable prescription drug benefit to Medicare.

For our neediest seniors, those who earn less than $11,900 a year, our bill would cover 100 percent of their prescription drug costs. They would pay no premiums, and Medicare would pick up the entire cost of their prescriptions.

About a third of our Medicare beneficiaries fall into this category. That's roughly 12 million seniors.

Those who earn more than $11,900 would pay premiums of $25 a month or less, depending on their income. And they would pay an affordable share of the cost of each prescription.

No senior would have to spend more than $4,000 a year out of their own pocket. Right now, about 3 million seniors are spending more than $4,000 a year out of their own pocket on prescriptions.

The two other bills of which I am a co-sponsor deal directly with the cost of prescription drugs. We must bring the cost of these drugs down. A miracle drug can't work miracles if no one can afford it.

As many of you know—and as most of the seniors in this country know—you can buy the same drug in the same bottle for a much cheaper price in Canada and other countries than you can in the U.S.

In Canada, you can buy Tamoxifen, the drug for breast cancer, for one-tenth what it costs in the U.S. Celebrex, which is used for arthritis, costs 79 cents a tablet in Canada, but $2.20 a tablet in the U.S. Those are two of many examples.

A bipartisan group of senators has introduced a bill to let drug stores and medical distributors buy U.S.-made drugs in Canada—where they are sold much more cheaply—and then resell them here in the U.S.

If our seniors could buy their drugs at the lower Canadian prices, they could save an estimated $38 billion a year.

Our seniors should be able to get their medications at the best price possible, and they shouldn't have to ride a bus to Canada to do it.

The other bill I am co-sponsoring that would help bring down the cost of prescription drugs is the Fair Advertising and Increased Research Act of 2002.

We have all seen the endless stream of ads on TV about the latest wonder drugs for high cholesterol of arthritis or cancer.

I have visions of that purple pill that keeps spinning into my living room and bedroom whenever the TV is on. You can't escape it.

You can't escape these ads. They are everywhere. We are drowning in them. And the millions of dollars the drug companies are spending on them is sending the price of prescriptions through the roof.

Our bill doesn't ban this TV advertising, but it does say to the drug companies: Spend as much on research as you do on advertising.

Our bill would limit the tax deduction a drug company can take for advertising expenses to no more than the amount they deduct for research and development costs.

Americans today are being forced to subsidize prescription drug advertising both when they pay their taxes and again when they go to the pharmacy to buy their prescriptions. That's not right, and our FAIR Act would help stop it.

We must do something soon. If I were to stay in the Senate as long as Senator Thurmond, I don't believe I would ever figure out how this wonderful place works.

I have come to accept that, just as I came to accept that the intricacies of cricket and even hockey escape me.

But I have known the infield fly rule since I was 12. And I also know what the men and women my age and a little older in middle America are saying and thinking.

What's that Latin phrase—the vox populi? Well, the vox populi of this nation's elderly are discouraged and displeased.

But they are not disorganized, and they are definitely not disenfranchised.

And if we don't show them some results instead of rhetoric pretty soon, they are going to come after us with their pitchforks and their pill cutters ... and something we in here fear even more: Their ballots. And who could blame them?

In 2000, both parties said prescription drugs was at the top of the list, at the front of the line. Our seniors have been waiting in line for a long time. Waiting as we debated many other worthwhile issues. Waiting, as we keep smiling at them, telling them: Now, be patient; you are next.

Do you know what makes people madder than anything? Making them wait in line for a long time and then, when they think they are just about to go to the front of that line, someone cuts in front of them. That is what we have been doing to our senior citizens. Every time we take up a new issue, no matter how good it is, every time we take up a new issue other than prescription drugs, we are bumping our seniors from the front of the line that they have been waiting in for years.

We cannot throw this issue into another election cycle. They will not stand for it. We cannot keep our seniors waiting in line through another election.

[Congressional Record: S4824]

" It is not a pretty picture. No matter who you send to Washington, for the most part smart and decent people, it is not going to change much because the individuals are not so much at fault as the rotten and decaying foundation of what is no longer a Republic. It is the system that stinks, and it is only going to get worse because that perfect balance our brilliant Founding Fathers put in place in 1787 no longer exists. "

REPEAL OF DIRECT
ELECTION OF SENATORS

April 28, 2004

Madam President, we live in perilous times. The leader of the free world's power has become so neutered he cannot, even with the support of the majority of the Senate, appoint highly 'qualified individuals endorsed by the American Bar to a Federal court. He cannot conduct a war without being torn to shreds by partisans with their eyes set, not on he defeat of our enemy but on the defeat of our President.

The Senate has become just one big, bad, ongoing joke, held hostage by special interests, and so impotent an 18-wheeler truck loaded with Viagra would do no good.

Andrew Young, one of the most thoughtful men in America, recently took a long and serious look at the Senate. He was thinking about making a race for it. After visiting Washington, he concluded that the Senate is composed of:

A bunch of pompous, old—and I won't use his word here, I would say "folks"—listening to people read statements they didn't even write and probably don't believe.

The House of Representatives, theoretically the closest of all the Federal Government to the people, cannot restrain its extravagant spending nor limit our spiraling debt, and incumbents are so entrenched you might as well call off 80 percent of the House races. There are no contests.

Most of the laws of the land, at least the most important and lasting ones, are made not by elected representatives of the people but by unelected, unaccountable legislators in black robes who churn out volumes of case law and hold their jobs for life. A half dozen dirty bombs the size of a small suitcase planted around the country could kill hundreds of thousands of our citizens and bring this Nation to its knees at any time, and yet we can't even build a fence along our border to keep out illegals because some nutty environmentalists say it will cause erosion.

This Government is in one hell of a mess. Frankly, as Rhett Butler said—my dear, very few people up here give a damn.

It is not funny. It is sad. It is tragic. And it can only get worse—much worse. What this Government needs is one of those extreme makeovers they have on television, and I am not referring to some minor nose job or a little botox here and there.

Congressional Quarterly recently devoted an issue to the mandate wars, with headlines blaring: "Unfunded Mandates Add to Woes, States Say; Localities Get the Bill for Beefed Up Security; Transportation Money Comes With Strings, and Medicare Stuck in Funding Squabbles," et cetera, et cetera, et cetera.

One would think that the much heralded Unfunded Mandate Reform Act of 1995 never passed. The National Conference of State Legislatures has set the unfunded mandate figure for the States at $33 billion for 2005. This, along with the budget problems they have been having for the last few years, has put States under the heel of a distant and unresponsive government. That is us. And it gives the enthusiastic tax raisers at the State level the very excuse they are looking for to dig deeper and deeper into the pockets of their taxpayers.

It is not a pretty picture. No matter who you send to Washington, for the most part smart and decent people, it is not going to change much because the individuals are not so much at fault as the rotten and decaying foundation of what is no longer a Republic. It is the system that stinks, and it is only going to get worse because that perfect balance our brilliant Founding Fathers put in place in 1787 no longer exists.

Perhaps, then, the answer is a return to the original thinking of those wisest of all men, and how they intended for this government to function. Federalism, for all practical purposes, has become to this generation of leaders, some vague philosophy of the past that is dead, dead, dead. It isn't even on life support. The line on that monitor went flat some time ago.

You see, the reformers of the early 1900s killed it dead and cremated the body when they allowed for the direct election of U.S. Senators.

Up until then, Senators were chosen by State legislatures, as James Madison and Alexander Hamilton had so carefully crafted.

Direct elections of Senators, as great and as good as that sounds, allowed Washington's special interests to call the shots, whether it is filling judicial vacancies, passing laws, or issuing regulations. The State governments aided in their own collective suicide by going along with that popular fad at the time.

Today it is heresy to even think about changing the system. But can you imagine those dreadful unfunded mandates being put on the States or a homeland security bill being torpedoed by the unions if Senators were still chosen by and responsible to the State legislatures?

Make no mistake about it. It is the special interest groups and their fundraising power that elect Senators and then hold them in bondage forever.

In the past five election cycles, Senators have raised over $1.5 billion for their election contests, not counting all the soft money spent on their behalf in other ways. Few would believe it, but the daily business of the Senate in fact is scheduled around fundraising.

The 17th Amendment was the death of the careful balance between State and Federal Government. As designed by that brilliant and very practical group of Founding Fathers, the two governments would be in competition with each other and neither could abuse or threaten the other. The election of Senators by the State legislatures was the lynchpin that guaranteed the interests of the States would be protected.

Today State governments have to stand in line because they are just another one of the many special interests that try to get Senators to listen to them, and they are at an extreme disadvantage because they have no PAC.

You know what the great historian Edward Gibbons said of the decline of the Roman Empire. I quote: "The fine theory of a republic insensibly vanished."

That is exactly what happened in 1913 when the State legislatures, except for Utah and Delaware, rushed pell-mell to ratify the popular 17th

Amendment and, by doing so, slashed their own throats and destroyed federalism forever. It was a victory for special-interest tyranny and a blow to the
power of State governments that would cripple them forever.

Instead of Senators who thoughtfully make up their own minds as they
did during the Senate's greatest era of Clay, Webster, and Calhoun, we now
have too many Senators who are mere cat's-paws for the special interests. It is
the Senate's sorriest of times in its long, checkered, and once glorious history.

Having now jumped off the Golden Gate Bridge of political reality,
before I hit the water and go splat, I have introduced a bill that would repeal
the 17th Amendment. I use the word "would," not "will," because I know it
doesn't stand a chance of getting even a single cosponsor, much less a single
vote beyond my own.

Abraham Lincoln, as a young man, made a speech in Springfield, IL, in
which he called our founding principles "a fortress of strength." Then he
went on to warn, and again I quote, that they "would grow more and more
dim by the silent artillery of time."

A wise man, that Lincoln, who understood and predicted all too well the
fate of our republican form of government. Too bad we didn't listen to him.

[Congressional Record: S4503]

" So, if I am asked why—with all the pressing

problems this Nation faces today—why am I pushing

these social issues and taking the Senate's valuable time,

I will answer: Because, it is of the highest importance.

Yes, there is a deficit to be concerned about in

this country, a deficit of decency. "

MORAL DECAY

February 12, 2004

The Old Testament prophet, Amos, was a sheep herder who lived back in the Judean hills, away from the larger cities of Bethlehem and Jerusalem. Compared to the intellectual urbanites like Isaiah and Jeremiah, Amos was just an unsophisticated country hick. But Amos had a unique grasp of political and social issues, and his poetic literary skill was among the best of all the prophets.

That familiar quote of Martin Luther King, Jr.:

"Justice will rush down like waters and righteousness like a mighty stream..."

Those are Amos's words.

Amos was the first to propose the concept of a universal God and not just some tribal deity. He also wrote that God demanded moral purity, not rituals and sacrifices.

This blunt-speaking moral conscience of his time warns, in Chapter 8, verse 11 of the Book of Amos, as if he were speaking to us today:

"The days will come, sayeth the Lord God, that I will send a famine in the land. Not a famine of bread or of thirst for water, but of hearing the word of the Lord.

"And they shall wander from sea to sea and from the north even to the east. They shall run to and fro to seek the word of the Lord, and shall not find it."

"A famine in the land," has anyone more accurately described the situation we face in America today? A famine of "hearing the word of the Lord." Some will say Amos was just an Old Testament prophet who lived 700 years before Christ.

That is true. So how about one of the most influential historians of modern times, Arnold Toynbee, who wrote the acclaimed 12-volume *A Study of History*. He once declared:

"Of the 22 civilizations that have appeared in history, 19 of them have collapsed when they reached the moral state America is in today."

Toynbee died in 1975, before seeing the worst that was yet to come. Yes, Arnold Toynbee saw the famine, "the famine of hearing the word of the Lord," whether it is removing a display of the Ten Commandments from a courthouse or of a nativity scene from a city square, whether it is eliminating prayer in the city schools or eliminating "under God" in the Pledge of Allegiance, whether it is making a mockery of the sacred institution of marriage between a man and a woman, or, yes, telecasting around the world made-in-the-USA filth masquerading as entertainment.

The culture of far left America was displayed in a startling way during the Super Bowl's now infamous half-time show, a show brought to us on behalf of the Value-Les Moonves and the pagan temple of Viacom-Babylon.

I asked the question yesterday: How many of you have ever run over a skunk with your car? I know the President has, somewhere over there around Frog Hollow. I have, many times. I can tell you that the stink stays around for a long time. You can take the car through a carwash and it is still there. So the scent of this event will long linger in the nostrils of America.

I am not talking just about an exposed mammary gland with a pull-tab attached to it. Really, no one should have been too surprised with that. Wouldn't you expect a bumping, humping, trashy routine entitled "I'm Going To Get You Naked" to end that way?

Does any responsible adult ever listen to the words of this rap-crap? I would quote you some of it, but the Sergeant at Arms would throw me out of this Chamber, as well he should.

Then there was that prancing, dancing, strutting, rutting guy, evidently suffering from jock itch because he kept yelling and grabbing his crotch. But, then, maybe there is a culture of crotch grabbing in this country I don't know about. But as bad as all that was, the thing that yanked my chain the hardest was seeing this ignoramus with his pointed head stuck up through a hole he had cut in the flag of the United States of America, screaming about having "a bottle of scotch and watching lots of crotch."

Think about that. This is the same flag to which we pledge allegiance. This is the same flag that is draped over coffins of dead young uniformed warriors, killed while protecting Kid Crock's boney butt. He should be tarred and feathered and ridden out of this country on a rail. You talk about a good reality show? That would be one.

The desire and will of this Congress to meaningfully do anything about any of these so-called social issues is nonexistent and embarrassingly disgraceful. The American people are waiting and growing impatient with us. They want something done.

I am pleased to be a cosponsor of S.J. Res. 26, along with Senator Allard and others, proposing an amendment to the Constitution of the United States relating to marriage; and S. 1558, the Liberties Restoration Act, which declares religious liberty rights in several ways, including the Pledge of Allegiance and the display of the Ten Commandments.

Today, I join Senator Shelby and others with the Constitution Restoration Act of 2004 that limits the jurisdiction of Federal courts in certain ways.

In doing so, I stand shoulder to shoulder, not only with my Senate cosponsors and Chief Justice Roy Moore of Alabama, but more importantly with our Founding Fathers in the conception of religious liberty and the terribly wrong direction our modern judiciary has taken us.

Everyone today seems to think the U.S. Constitution expressly provides for separation of church and state. I guess you could ask any 10 people if that is not so and I will bet you most of them will say, well, sure that is so. And some would point out that is in the First Amendment.

Wrong. Read it. It says:

"Congress shall make no law respecting an establishment of religion or prohibiting the free exercise thereof."

Where is the word "separate"? Where are the words "church" and "state"?

They are not there; never have been, never intended to be. Read the Congressional Record during the 4-month period in 1789 when the amendment was being framed in Congress. Clearly their intent was to prohibit a single denomination in exclusion of all others, whether it was Anglican or Catholic or some other.

I highly recommend a great book entitled *Original Intent* by David Barton.

It really gets into how the actual Members of Congress, who drafted the First Amendment, expected basic Biblical principles and values to be present throughout public life and society, not separate from it.

It was Alexander Hamilton who pointed out that "judges should be bound down by strict rules and precedents, which serve to define and point out their duty."

"Bound down." That is exactly what is needed to be done. There was not a single precedent cited when school prayer was struck down in 1962.

These judges who legislate instead of adjudicate do it without being responsible to one single solitary voter for their actions.

Among the signers of the Declaration of Independence was a brilliant young physician from Pennsylvania named Benjamin Rush.

When Rush was elected to that First Continental Congress, his close friend Benjamin Franklin told him "We need you ... we have a great task before us, assigned to us by Providence."

Today, 228 years later there is still a great task before us assigned to us by Providence. Our Founding Fathers did not shirk their duty and we can do no less.

By the way, Benjamin Rush was once asked a question that has long interested this Senator from Georgia in particular. Dr. Rush was asked, Are you a democrat or an aristocrat? And the good doctor answered, "I am neither". "I am a Christocrat. I believe He, alone, who created and redeemed man is qualified to govern him."

That reply of Benjamin Rush is just as true today in the year of our Lord 2004 as it was in the Year of Our Lord 1776.

So, if I am asked why—with all the pressing problems this Nation faces today—why am I pushing these social issues and taking the Senate's valuable time, I will answer: Because, it is of the highest importance. Yes, there is a deficit to be concerned about in this country, a deficit of decency.

So, as the sand empties through my hourglass at warp speed—and with my time running out in this Senate and on this Earth—I feel compelled to speak out for I truly believe that at times like this, silence is not golden. It is yellow.

[Congressional Record: S1271-1272]

" But I need to know tonight where in the U.S. Constitution does it say the President's nominees for the judiciary must have a supermajority to be confirmed? Where does it say that? I have searched high and low for that clause and that provision. I cannot find it. Maybe these old 71-year-old eyes are getting kind of dim. Perhaps I need a magnifying glass. "

JUDICIAL FILIBUSTERS

October 30, 2003

Mr. President, I rise today to talk about a good and brave man from the State of Mississippi, Judge Charles Pickering. I also rise today to talk about a judicial nominating process that is badly broken and out of control. Judge Charles Pickering has been victimized by inaccurate race baiting and political trash talk of the news media, Members of Congress, and Washington's liberal elite. Judge Pickering's critics continue to unfairly label him a racist and segregationist. Nothing could be further from the truth.

Judge Pickering has worked courageously in difficult times—difficult times many in this body could not hope to understand—to eliminate racial disparities in Mississippi and the South. My good friend, former Governor William Winter of Mississippi, a Democrat and one of the South's most respected progressives, came to Washington to support Judge Pickering's nomination. Sadly, Governor Winter's praise and firsthand account of Pickering's true record fell on deaf ears by most Capitol Hill Democrats.

Charles Pickering deserves an up-or-down vote on his nomination, as does another fine nominee who has been treated in the same shameful manner, Justice Janice Rogers Brown of California. On both of these nominees, I fear we are about to cave in once again to the left-leaning special interest groups. These special interest groups, like termites, have come out of the woodwork to denounce Justice Brown simply because she is an African American who also happens to be conservative. Never mind that Justice Brown is intelligent, articulate, chock-full of common sense, and highly qualified to serve on the Federal appeals court bench. Never mind that in 1998, 76 percent of Californians voted to retain Justice Brown. That is a job approval rating most of us could only dream of.

The special interest groups don't care about any of that. They don't want to hear how qualified Justice Brown and Judge Pickering are, or how much the voters like the job they have done.

No, their only mission is to assassinate these good people's character and to take them down one way or another because they fear they won't cater to their liberal agenda. They are right; they won't. These fine nominees are much too independent and much too intelligent to be held hostage to anyone's extreme agenda. Or as Thomas Sowell wrote of Justice Brown in a column headlined "A Lynch Mob Takes Aim at Judicial Pick":

"What really scares the left about Brown is that she has guts as well as brains. She won't weaken or waver."

So they can publish all the racist cartoons they want and they can demonize Judge Pickering and brutally and callously reduce Justice Brown to tears at her committee meeting. They can sneeringly accuse them both of being outside the mainstream. But President Bush knows and the voters of California and Mississippi know, and the majority of this Senate knows, Charles Pickering and Janice Rogers Brown are not the ones who are outside the mainstream. The ones who are completely out of touch are the special interest groups that have taken this nominating process hostage and those in this body who have aided and abetted their doing so.

Speaking of lynch mobs, my all-time favorite movie is *To Kill a Mockingbird*. In the movie's key scene, you may remember, Atticus Finch, a lawyer who is raising two small children, is defending a black man unjustly accused of rape. That lynch mob also tries to take justice into its own hands. Atticus confronts them at the jailhouse door. His daughter Scout joins him and sees that the leader of the mob is someone she knows. She calls to him by name: "Hey, Mr. Cunningham. Remember me? You are Walter's daddy. Walter is a good boy. Tell him I said hello."

After a dramatic pause, Mr. Cunningham turns away and says to the mob: "Let's go home, boys."

This group, bent on injustice, was turned aside by a small girl who appealed to them as individuals.

My friends in this Chamber, I know you, and I appeal to each of you as individuals, as fathers, mothers, colleagues and friends. Most of you were taught in Sunday school to do unto others as you would have them do unto you. This is not treating someone as you would want to be treated yourself. This extreme partisanship and deliberately planned obstructionism has gone on long enough in this body. I wish we could do away with the 60-vote rule that lets a small minority rule this Chamber and defeat the majority, reversing the rule of free government everywhere; everywhere, that is, except in the Senate.

[Congressional Record: S13546]

November 12, 2003

Mr. President, I stand here proudly next to a copy of the U.S. Constitution. It is a document that has stood the test of time. It is a document that is revered throughout the world. As a history professor, I have read it many times. But I need to know tonight where in the U.S. Constitution does it say the President's nominees for the judiciary must have a supermajority to be confirmed? Where does it say that? I have searched high and low for that clause and that provision. I cannot find it. Maybe these old 71-year-old eyes are getting kind of dim. Perhaps I need a magnifying glass.

I seek. I search. I hunt in vain. For is it not there. Even if I had the eye of an eagle I could not find it because it is simply not there.

No, the U.S. Constitution says only the Senate is to advise and consent on the President's nominees. Somehow that has been twisted and perverted into this unmitigated mess we have today where 59 votes out of 100 cannot pass anything because 41 votes out of 100 can defeat anything. Explain that to Joe Sixpack in the Wal-Mart parking lot.

Explain that to this man, James Madison, who wrote that Constitution. He predicted and he feared some day someone would try to finagle this system, that they would try to plot and conspire and pervert the process in just the way they have. James Madison warned about this in Federalist Paper 58. He said: If that should happen, "The fundamental principle of free government would be reversed. It would be no longer the majority that would rule. The power would be transferred to the minority."

But don't just take my word for it. Look at others who are far smarter, far wiser than I will ever be and how they have expressed the kinds of things that are going on around here.

On June 1, 1950, a brave woman who was then the Senator from the State of Maine, Margaret Chase Smith, gave one of the most courageous speeches ever given on the floor of this Senate. It has been called the "declaration of conscience" speech. Senator Smith questioned what was happening at that time in the Senate. It was not about filibusters but, make no mistake, it was about intrigue, and it was about character assassination.

Let me give you a few excerpts from Senator Smith:

"The United States Senate has long enjoyed worldwide respect as the greatest deliberative body in the world. But recently that deliberative character has too often been debased to the level of a forum of hate and character assassination sheltered by the shield of congressional immunity."

She went on:

"It is ironic that we senators can during debate in the Senate [and in committee], directly or indirectly, by any form of words, impute to any American who is not a Senator any conduct or any motive unworthy or becoming an American—and without that non-senator American having any legal redress against us."

She went on:

"It is strange that we can verbally attack anyone without restraint and with full protection, and yet we hold ourselves above the same type of criticism here on the Senate floor. Surely, the United States Senate is big enough to take self-criticism and self-appraisal. Surely we should be able to take the same kind of character attacks we dish out to others."

She continued:

"I think it is high time for the United States Senate and its members to do some real soul searching and to weigh our consciences as to the manner in which we are performing our duty for the people of America and the manner in which we are using or abusing our individual powers and privileges.

"I think it is high time we remembered that we have sworn to uphold and defend the Constitution. I think it is high time that we remembered that the Constitution, as amended, speaks not only of the freedom of speech but also of trial by jury instead of trial by accusation."

So said Margaret Chase Smith in 1950.

Let me tell you what Thomas Sowell, in his recent book *The Quest for Cosmic Justice* writes about the role of a judge:

"The traditional conception of the role of judges was expressed thousands of years ago by Aristotle, who said that a judge should 'be allowed to decide as few things as possible.' His discretion should be limited to 'such points as the lawgiver has not already defined for him.' "

A judge cannot "do justice" directly in the cases before him. This view was strongly expressed in a small episode in the life of Justice Oliver Wendell Holmes. After having lunch [one day] with Judge Learned Hand, Holmes entered his carriage to be driven away. As he left, Judge Hand's parting salute was: "Do justice, sir, do justice." Holmes ordered the carriage stopped. "That is not my job," Holmes said to Judge Hand. "It is my job to apply the law."

Elsewhere Holmes wrote that his primary responsibility as a judge was "to see that the game is played according to the rules whether I like them or not."

Lastly, I want to quote a Georgian named Phil Kent. In his book *The Dark Side of Liberalism*, he takes the liberal argument in this controversy and states it. He says:

"The United States [according to the liberals, according to the Democrats in this debate we are in today] comprises diverse people and cultures. As such, judges should have the power to change laws when circumstances dictate. The U.S. Constitution is a document in flux, and is many times irrelevant in modern society. Therefore, federal judges should be chosen on the basis of their views or the positions of their issues and should be tested on their ideologies."

That is what the Democrats have been saying to us in all this debate. Then Kent answered that premise:

"We are a nation of laws, not of men. Our government is constitutional, not political. Our highest court is the arbiter of constitutional controversies, and the protector of unalienable rights. As former President Ronald Reagan underscored, 'Freedom is indivisible—there is no "s" on the end of it. You can erode freedom, diminish it, but you cannot divide it and choose to keep some freedoms while giving up others.' "

Ignoring the law, whether seen as politically expedient or ideologically sound, suggests that the courts are merely devices to be used to change policy.

The courts, however, are partners with specific duties separate and apart from lawmaking and law execution. We've missed that point as a nation for too long, to our great peril.

That brings me to this map of the United States. I ask you to look at the faces on this map. They are the faces of America. These are the faces of America. There is Miguel Estrada, who spoke little English when he came to this country as a teenage immigrant from Honduras. But a few years later, this immigrant graduated magna cum laude from Columbia College in New York and from Harvard Law School. He clerked for Justice Anthony Kennedy on the highest court in this land, the U.S. Supreme Court. He continued to soar with a very distinguished law career. Yet the Democrats in this Chamber have decided this man could not even have an up-or-down vote. It is a shame, and it is a disgrace.

There is Bill Pryor, a devout Catholic and a southerner who grew up in a house where both John F. Kennedy and Ronald Reagan were revered. He graduated magna cum laude from Northeast Louisiana University and Tulane University Law School. He also has had a very distinguished law career, including winning statewide election twice as Alabama's attorney general. Yet the Democrats in this Senate will not give him an up-or-down vote.

Then there is Charles Pickering, another southerner, a grandfather, a courageous and a deeply religious man. He graduated at the top of his law school class at the University of Mississippi, served in elective office for 12 years, practiced law for 30 years, and has served this country ably on the U.S. District Court since 1990. Yet the Democrats in this Senate refuse to give Judge Pickering an up-or-down vote.

There is Priscilla Owen, who grew up on a farm in rural Texas and later rose to win election to the Supreme Court of Texas. Along the way she graduated in the top of her class at Baylor University Law School and practiced law for 17 years. In her successful reelection bid to the Supreme Court in 2000, every major newspaper in Texas endorsed her. Yet in this Senate, this woman cannot get an up-or-down vote.

Finally, there is Janice Rogers Brown. I have spent a lot of time with this woman. I have read dozens of her speeches. I love and admire her. The daughter of an Alabama sharecropper who rose to serve on the California Supreme Court, she attended segregated schools until she was in high school and decided to become a lawyer after seeing African-American attorneys in the civil rights movement praised for their courage. In 1998, 76 percent of Californians voted to retain Justice Brown, an approval rating most of us can only dream of. Yet this African-American woman will not be given an up-or-down vote because the Democrats in this Chamber refuse to let her do it. They are standing in the doorway and they have a sign: Conservative African-American women need not apply, and if you have the temerity to do so, your reputation will be shattered and your dignity will be shredded. Gal, you will be lynched.

These are the faces of America, men and women who pulled themselves up, who worked hard, who played by the rules, and excelled in the field of law, and now all of their hard work and success has landed them in the doorway of the Senate, and each one of them is having that door slammed in their faces. The very least they deserve, the very least they deserve is an up-or-down vote. Surely, in the name of all that is fair and reasonable, surely, in the name of James Madison, surely in the United States of America in 2003, that is not too much to ask, just an up-or-down vote, just an up-or-down vote, just an up-or-down vote.

[Congressional Record: S14578-14579]

"If these higher CAFE standards are applied to pickups, they will be made unaffordable for many, and unsafe for all, and that will hurt those pickup pops. It will hurt the working man. It will hurt rural America."

CAFE Fuel Standards

March 6, 2002

Madam President, I rise today in defense of that great American workhorse: The pickup truck. I am proud to sponsor, along with my friend, Senator Gramm of Texas, an amendment that would exempt all pickup trucks from the higher CAFE standards that have been proposed.

This is a very simple and short amendment. Pickups are now required to meet a standard of 20.7 miles per gallon, and our amendment would simply freeze pickups at that standard. All pickups would be exempt from any higher mileage standard proposed in this legislation.

Some have said we should only exempt the very largest pickups from the higher standards. That would only cover a small percentage of the pickups that are on the road, and I do not think that is good enough. Our amendment says all pickups will be exempt from the higher CAFE standards.

We absolutely should not impose these higher mileage standards on our pickups. We absolutely should not impose the undue safety risk and extra cost of these CAFE standards on our farmers, our rural families, and our small businesses that rely so heavily on the pickup.

We have had a lot of conversation about the state of the economy these days, and we hang on every word of Alan Greenspan, Robert Rubin, and the like, about the recession and when we are coming out of it. I knew a fellow back in Georgia. He did not have a Ph.D. in economics; he would have thought Ph.D. stood for "post hole digger." But he was one of the wisest men I ever knew. He told me years ago that if you really want to know when times are bad, take notice of the number of people having to sell their pickups. Look at the ads in the paper and the "for sale" signs in the yards. The more you see, the worse it is because pickups are the very symbol of the working man. As the pickup goes, so does the working man and the very heart of this country.

Madam President, a pickup truck has two ends to it: A working end and a thinking end. Of course, the working end is the engine in the front. I would like to tell you about the thinking end in the back.

I submit that the back of a pickup is the think tank of rural America. I suspect more problems have been solved on the tailgates of pickup trucks after a long day's work than have been solved anywhere.

I do not rise to speak often in this hallowed Chamber. I am still learning the complexities of being a Senator. I envy my learned colleagues who can speak with such great assurance on so many subjects. But, Madam President, on this one you can trust this man from the mountains of North Georgia. If this amendment fails, the tailgates of rural America are going to drop, and it will be a clank that will reverberate from now through November because then the conversation at the end of the day on the back of a pickup as the Sun goes down will not be about the farm or the family or the State or the Nation; the subject will be how to get rid of us in the next election.

Every election year we talk a lot about all those soccer moms out there and how they vote in such high percentages. Well, there is another group out there that votes in a very high percentage. They are the pickup pops. In fact, I would bet pickup pops go to the polls in higher percentages than any other Democratic group out there, and they also have long memories.

If these higher CAFE standards are applied to pickups, they will be made unaffordable for many, and unsafe for all, and that will hurt those pickup pops. It will hurt the working man. It will hurt rural America.

We are big on acronyms in Congress, and quite frankly they can be a little deceiving and confusing. I cannot even keep up with all of them. When we talk about CAFE and CAFE standards, most folks think we are talking about restaurants.

People in rural America also understand what an acronym is, and I think on this issue they would say that "pickup," P-I-C-K-U-P, is an acronym for "People in Congress Keep Us Perplexed." Let us not keep them perplexed anymore.

One of the first things I noticed when I came to Washington, DC is that you hardly ever see a pickup. They are scarce in Washington, DC, but they are not scarce outside the beltway, out there in middle America.

I want to show this chart. In 1999, pickup trucks accounted for almost 18 percent of all registered vehicles in this country. In 29 States, these red and blue States—that is more than half of our States, of course—pickups amounted to as much as 20 to 37 percent of all the registered vehicles. In the year 2000, drivers in this country bought 3.18 million pickup trucks. That makes pickups the third most popular choice of vehicle for American drivers.

So pickups may not be prevalent in Washington, DC, but pickups are popular across the rest of America. When all this talk about CAFE started last year, I got worried Washington was going to stick it to the pickup owners of this Nation, so I tried to write a song about it. I am no Orrin Hatch, but I tried to write a song about it with my good friend, Jack Clement, in Nashville. It is called the "Talking Pickup Truck Blues." I will spare everyone the agony of my singing, but I want to share one verse. It goes something like this:

"Sure, an SUV is classy travel, but it ain't much good for hauling gravel, or hay seed or bovine feces. So please do not make my pickup truck an endangered species."

Now, I will be the first to admit that song has not climbed to the top of the charts, but here is the point we are making: Do not mess with the working machine of the American road. Do not mess with pickups. Farmers depend on them. Families in rural America depend on them. Small businesses across this country depend on them, small businesses such as construction companies and home builders.

One of the greatest economic engines we have in this country is the housing industry. You can go to any construction site across America and see at least a half dozen pickups. Plumbers drive them. Electricians drive them. Painters drive them. Carpenters drive them. Raise the cost of a pickup truck and more than just pickup owners will be harmed; entire industries will be hurt—the housing industry and others that rely heavily on pickups.

Folks buy pickups not because they are affordable and they are safe.

They buy them because they get the job done, whatever that job may be, whether it is pulling a trailer full of cattle or hauling lumber to a construction site or driving on gravel and dirt roads in rural America. There are times when only a pickup will do.

So I urge my colleagues, who represent the millions of pickup owners across this country, when this amendment comes up at a later date to vote for this amendment. We must exempt the American workers, the pickup truck, from these higher CAFE standards.

Like the last verse in my song goes:

"So help us, Lord, and let there be a little wisdom in D.C."

[Congressional Record: S1588]

" I want to save this game for those who love it as I do and for those who will come after us. I do not want to see our national pastime become our national once-upon-a-time. "

MAJOR LEAGUE
BASEBALL

July 23, 2002

Mr. President, today I share with my colleagues a resolution that
calls on the Federal Mediation and Conciliation Service to exert
its best efforts to cause the Major League Baseball Players Association and
the owners of the teams of Major League Baseball to enter into a contract to
continue to play professional baseball games without engaging in any coercive conduct that interferes with the playing of scheduled professional baseball games.

Folks don't agree on much around this place. But, I think we can all
agree that baseball as we've known it is in deep trouble.

Billion dollar owners and multi-million dollar players refusing to come
together and do what's right for the game.

Steroid use rampant, according to an article in *Sports Illustrated*.

And the best Senator Dorgan could get out of a June hearing from the
Players Association Executive Director was for him to say "We'll have a frank
and open discussion" on the topic.

But the big problem is that the player's labor contract expired last year and the negotiations on a new deal are going nowhere.

There have been eight different labor agreements and each time there was a work stoppage.

The last time the owners and players tried to renew their contract back in 1994, it took a 232-day shutdown of the game, including canceling the World Series for the first time in 90 years, to finally get an agreement.

Hall of Famer and U.S. Senator Jim Bunning has an op-ed piece in this morning's *New York Times*. He writes, "The last strike nearly killed the game. I am afraid the next one will."

There are many problems. Only five out of thirty teams made a profit last season. That means 25 ended up in the red. The extreme ran from the Yankees collecting $217.8 million and the Montreal Expos $9.8 million.

The average player today, the average player, makes more than $2 million a year.

Ever since Abner Doubleday invented the game, a game is played until one team wins. That was part of the enchantment of the game: theoretically it could go on forever. Unless, that is, a commissioner calls it off and goes to dinner.

Ever since baseball was declared as entertainment instead of a business in a 1922 Supreme Court decision that gave the owners exemptions from laws against collusion and other monopolistic activities, we have probably been headed to this day. These anti-trust exemptions give owners tremendous power and any proposals to change it, like Rep. John Conyers tried to do not too long ago, have gone nowhere.

And, we're not proposing that today, I'm not even sure I'm for that. I happen to think that it would kill the minor leagues.

And right now, these 160 teams are playing some of the purest baseball being played today.

So what do we do? Here's how I see it.

What would any of us do if we saw a loved one, someone you grew up with and loved like a member of your family, with a pistol in his hand, loaded with the safety off and aimed at their temple?

What if you had only a few seconds before that close personal friend blew his brains out? I'd try to stop him. And I think you would too. I'd lurch for the pistol and try to take it away from him by whatever force necessary. I'd do just about anything to save his life.

I could go on with this analogy, but I think you get the picture.

For sixty summers I've followed the game of baseball. I live for the early days of February when the catchers and pitchers report for spring training.

And when the World Series ends in the late fall, I might as well be hibernating in a cave during the winter, or serving in the Senate, because my life is so empty.

But, I digress. Back to saving the life of that good friend about to blow his brains out.

That's what this resolution attempts to do.

Its purpose is to inject the Federal Government, with all its persuasive powers, into this dispute. Hopefully, with the end result of preventing the baseball players from striking and shutting down major league baseball.

I want to save this game for those who love it as I do and for those who will come after us. I do not want to see our national pastime become our national once-upon-a-time.

[Congressional Record: S7231-7232]

" I would never want to look a family
member in the eye and know that I did not do
everything possible to prevent such a prosecution
because of concern over world perception,
or offending their governments. "

INTERNATIONAL
CRIMINAL COURT

December 7, 2001

I would like to thank the distinguished senior Senator from North Carolina for his leadership and dedication in crafting this important legislation. I am proud to cosponsor it with him. He has worked hard with the Bush administration to write a bill that meets the President's approval, and I commend him for doing so. Senator Helms outlined the details on what this legislation is intended to do, so I will just make some brief comments on why I believe it is so important.

As Senator Helms stated, this legislation is designed to protect American troops and officials from the potential of illegitimate and politicized prosecutions under the auspices of an International Criminal Court. When just 13 more nations ratify the Rome Treaty, the International Criminal Court will be empowered, and Americans could be subject to its prosecutorial authority. This could happen even though the United States has not ratified the treaty.

We ask a lot of our military. They are at risk right now in Afghanistan. They are stretched to the limit, and are engaged in missions around the globe that include peacekeeping and humanitarian efforts.

In the conduct of these missions, we must provide them the tools to succeed. Exposing our troops to ICC prosecutions is tantamount to not adequately equipping them for the mission. Rules of engagement for many military missions are complex enough—our military doesn't need to be further burdened by the specter of the ICC when making critical deadly force decisions.

I have heard some of the arguments against this legislation. Some think it demonstrates U.S. arrogance and a unilateralist attitude. Others believe it somehow compromises our commitment to the promotion of human rights and the prosecution of war crimes. I appreciate those concerns, but in my opinion, the well-being and protection of our military trumps those arguments every time.

We should be concerned over world perception in terms of our commitment to addressing war crimes, genocide, and other human rights issues. However, I don't believe any reasonable government could accuse us of not being the world's leader in all of these areas. The suggestion that the United States is not supportive of human rights because we refuse to ratify a questionable treaty just doesn't compute.

Some would advocate that we should ratify this treaty and try to fix its deficiencies after the ICC is created. That is laughable to me. How many of us would sign a contract for anything before negotiating the details? It makes more sense to have this proposed legislation as an insurance policy and then negotiate, rather than negotiate without it and potentially place our people at risk.

I remind my distinguished colleagues of the concern we all had when the Chinese held our EP-3 crew for 11 days. And they were only detained—not prosecuted. Now imagine American service members being subjected an unfair ICC prosecution without U.S. consent. This could happen to some those brave troops that are eating dust and risking their lives in Afghanistan to protect America. I would never want to look a family member in the eye and know that I did not do everything possible to prevent such a prosecution because of concern over world perception, or offending their governments. This legislation seeks to provide that much-deserved protection.

I encourage my colleagues to support this important legislation. As responsible lawmakers, we are obligated to provide them this legislative protection.

[Congressional Record: S12614]

June 6, 2002

Madam President, I rise to support the American Servicemembers' Protection Act amendment. I am very pleased to join with my distinguished colleague from Virginia in support of this legislation, just as I was pleased to join with Senator Helms in working with him and his staff on its behalf.

It might be worth noting that Senator Helms made a determined effort and has been making a determined effort to pass this legislation. I think that is very admirable, and I would like to commend him again for his leadership and wish him well.

I will not restate the details of this amendment since Senator Warner has already articulated them so well, but I would like to make a few brief points.

As Senator Warner mentioned, the Senate passed legislation similar to this amendment as part of the 2002 Defense appropriations bill. The final vote was 78 to 21, which constituted a clear majority of this Senate. Unfortunately, the conference committee missed an opportunity to have this protective legislation in place before the International Criminal Court was ratified earlier this year. Now the International Criminal Court becomes effective on July 1, and American servicemembers, officials, and citizens will then potentially be subject to a court to which we are not a party.

That is why, in a nutshell, this legislation is so important. We need some degree of protection for our men and women in uniform and for other officials who sacrifice so much for our Nation.

This amendment is appropriately entitled the American Servicemembers' Protection Act because our war on terrorism could put our military at risk of politicized prosecutions by the International Criminal Court. Other brave Americans who serve this country are also at risk, and this legislation will protect them as well. I believe that as elected lawmakers we are obligated to safeguard them from this potential threat just as we would from threats on the battlefield. I also believe it is important for our military to know that Congress will not stand idly by while this questionable Court comes into existence.

Make no mistake about it, our servicemembers are very aware of the importance of this pending legislation. We must send them the clear message that they have our full support.

I can guarantee that if we do not get this done, and done soon, we will look back and regret our inaction. I, for one, do not want to look a parent in the eye and explain why their son or daughter is being subjected to an international court on a trumped up charge of war crimes.

The administration supports this amendment, as Senator Warner said, and so should we. Let us do the right thing again, as we did in December, and pass this amendment.

[Congressional Record: S5139-5140]

" We must strike the viper's nest—even if the viper is not there. We know that the Taliban and the Government of Afghanistan have nurtured Osama bin Laden for years. The diabolical plot was probably hatched there. Certainly similar plots have been. And it is time for us to respond. "

SEPTEMBER 11TH

September 12, 2001

The victims and the loved ones of this horrible act of war should be in our prayers. The perpetrators and those who give them shelter should be in our bombsights.

After Pearl Harbor, the Japanese remarked that the "sleeping giant has been awakened." I pray that "the sleeping giant" has again been awakened, and that we are ready to change the way we do things.

For too long, after terrorist attacks have happened, it seems America's first and foremost interest has been to please our friends, and then, if permitted, punish our enemies.

After yesterday and from here on out, that must be reversed. America's first and foremost interest must be to punish our enemies, and then, if possible, please our friends.

Our response should not only be swift but it must be sustained. As I said yesterday, our will as a country has been tested. Too often in the past terrorist attacks have not been answered as forcefully as they should have been. Oh, yes, there has been indignation, even outrage. There has been wringing of hands and sad talk. We have shaken our collective heads in dismay, sighed over our cocktails, then have gone home, had a nice dinner and got into a comfortable bed, feeling safe and secure that it is not going to happen here, that it is not going to happen to us.

Well, it has happened to us. It has happened here. Our world has been turned upside down. It will never be the same again, and it shouldn't.

We must strike the viper's nest—even if the viper is not there. We know that the Taliban and the Government of Afghanistan have nurtured Osama bin Laden for years. The diabolical plot was probably hatched there. Certainly similar plots have been. And it is time for us to respond.

I say, bomb the hell out of them. If there is collateral damage, so be it. They certainly found our American civilians to be expendable.

I also believe that we could immediately turn our attention to the security of our airlines. There is a large pool of willing ex-military personnel out there who possess the rudimentary skills to be effective, temporary air marshals if given a crash training course on the basic requirements of that job. Another option may be to have active duty military personnel do that job.

We should also install "communications hardware" aboard each aircraft that would let pilots make emergency transmissions to air traffic controllers. With today's "star wars" capability, I believe it is possible to outfit each aircraft with an emergency transponder combined with an "open mike" type system that would be strictly for one-way communication from aircraft to air traffic control. The pilot or crew members could push a button, much similar to a silent bank alarm, that would instantly alert authorities. It could also serve as a hidden microphone in the cockpit or in the passenger cabins.

Those are some of my thoughts today for whatever they are worth at this terrible time.

To paraphrase President Roosevelt, this Nation will endure as it has endured, but we must change the way we do business drastically.

[Congressional Record: S9321]

October 10, 2001

Mr. President, I rise today to offer thanks and praise for a world leader who has been as stalwart and as loyal an ally for the United States as anyone could ever ask.

These past few weeks, British Prime Minister Tony Blair has gone above and beyond the call of duty for America. He has left no doubt that we will be able to count on him and his country over the long haul.

To paraphrase his own words, he was with us at the first and he will stay with us to the last.

He was there in the gallery of the House of Representatives when President Bush made his moving and forceful speech to this Nation in a joint session of this Congress.

He was there at Ground Zero in New York City, witnessing the destruction with his own eyes and mourning what he called "the slaughter of thousands of innocents."

He was there in Pakistan, near the dangerous heart of this war, reassuring a nervous Pakistani President that he made the right decision in choosing the United States over the Taliban regime.

Since September 11, Tony Blair has served valiantly as our voluntary ambassador to the world.

In London, Berlin, Paris, New York, Washington, Brussels, Moscow, Islamabad, New Delhi, and Geneva, Blair has rallied international leaders and built a coalition of support for the United States. He has done so with a diplomacy, eloquence and strong resolve reminiscent of Winston Churchill during his finest hours.

In his latest brilliant stroke, Blair acted swiftly when he saw Osama bin Laden's videotaped speech Sunday night. Blair immediately summoned a reporter from the Arabic network to his office at 10 Downing Street and taped his own strong rebuttal to bin Laden. It aired on the same day, on the same Arabic network.

It should not be surprising that Blair would rise to the occasion as ably and powerfully as he has. The British have a tough, resolute attitude when it comes to defending themselves. They are willing to take risks on the battlefield. They are willing to risk casualties for the greater good. They are the ones you want on your side in times like these.

He was with us at the first, and he will stay with us to the last, he said. For that, we owe Tony Blair our deepest gratitude. We could not ask any more of him.

[Congressional Record: S10423]

" With these new threats, the American public has uniformly called for giving the pilots every measure of protection possible in order to make our skies safer. But there are some folks who are leery of putting their trust in our Nation's pilots. I cannot understand the logic that says we can trust someone with a Boeing 747 in bad weather, but we cannot trust that same person with a Glock 9 millimeter. "

ARMED AIRLINE PILOTS

September 5, 2002

Our airline pilots are among the most highly trained professionals in all of the American workforce. Every day millions of Americans put their lives in the hands of airline pilots, and we have great reason to give them our trust.

Thanks to literally thousands and thousands of hours of training, commercial airline pilots have made aviation our Nation's safest form of public transportation. But since September 11, our Nation's pilots are faced with a grave new danger: Homicidal fanatics who think nothing of using our airplanes to kill themselves and as many Americans as they can.

With these new threats, the American public has uniformly called for giving the pilots every measure of protection possible in order to make our skies safer.

But there are some folks who are leery of putting their trust in our Nation's pilots. I cannot understand the logic that says we can trust someone with a Boeing 747 in bad weather, but we cannot trust that same person with a Glock 9 millimeter.

The folks who oppose arming pilots say we should put our trust elsewhere. We have heard about making the doors stronger. We have heard about security screeners. The Senator from California talked about the recent examples in the airports in New York where so many went through with things that they should not have had in their luggage. We all know how that is. We travel. We see it. Deep down we know it is a screening process that our Nation's Transportation Security Administration's own studies show fails one out of every four times. So let's face it, if our pilots were failing one out of every four landings, America would not be putting our trust in them to keep us safe.

Our Nation's air safety plan has multiple levels, from little steps such as banning nail clippers, all the way up to authorizing military fighter aircraft to shoot down a commercial jetliner filled with innocent passengers.

Why is there not—somewhere between banning nail clippers and shooting down the plane, somewhere between those two extremes—some room for allowing a trained pilot to use a handgun to defend the cockpit?

Some critics have worried what might happen if terrorists got hold of the gun, to which I would answer: Nothing worse than if terrorists got control of the aircraft. Others wonder what happens if a bullet goes astray in the fight with a terrorist. Could it damage the aircraft? I would answer: Yes, but not nearly as much as a missile that would be fired at the aircraft if terrorists took control.

If you have any doubts about how the American public feels about this subject, ask them this question: If you had to choose between flying on an airline with pilots who were armed to protect the cockpit and an airline whose pilots were unarmed, which would you choose? I am convinced they would overwhelmingly choose to fly with armed pilots, and I am just as convinced that terrorists would prefer to fly with defenseless pilots.

That is why I am a cosponsor of this bipartisan amendment to train and arm our Nation's airline pilots. I, for one, trust our Nation's pilots to keep me safe when I fly. But I want to give them more than just my trust. I want to give them the training and the tools they need to keep all Americans safe in the air.

[Congressional Record: S8275]

"When it comes to choosing between an aged, arthritic civil service system filled with stumbling blocks and booby traps, or an agile agency that is nimble and responsive on the other, this American stands with his President. I have made my choice. When it comes to choosing between real homeland security that protects somebody's life or homebound insecurity that protects somebody's job, this American stands with his President."

HOMELAND SECURITY

September 18, 2002

Madam President, very shortly we will be back on the subject of homeland security. As this debate on homeland security goes on, I hope no one will forget that it is being held in the shadows of the fallen towers of the World Trade Center.

The smoldering fires may have gone out, the acrid smell may no longer burn our nostrils, the strains of "Amazing Grace" from the bagpipes may no longer fill the air, but, make no mistake about it, the need to protect this country and prevent this from ever happening again is just as urgent.

How does the Senate meet this, one of the greatest challenges of our time? I will tell you.

We talk and talk and talk. Then we pause to go out on the steps of the Capitol to sing "God Bless America" with our best profile to the camera. Then we come back inside and show our worst profile to the country.

I have not seen many cloture resolutions I did not like. I can't remember the last time I voted against one because I am almost always in favor of speeding things up around here.

Too often, the Senate reminds me of Will Shakespeare's words:

"Tomorrow and tomorrow and tomorrow

"Creeps in this petty pace from day to day."

But the cloture vote that is before us now is one that I cannot support. We have wasted so many precious days, days that we could ill afford to waste, days that gave our enemies more time to plot their next attack. And now, all of a sudden, we want to invoke cloture to stop the debate in its tracks.

Well, I will vote "no." Because, make no mistake about it, invoking cloture will prevent this Senate from having a choice, a choice between a bill the President will sign and one that he will veto.

We must give the President the flexibility to respond to terrorism on a moment's notice. He has to be able to shift resources, including personnel, at the blink of an eye.

So why do we hold so dear a personnel system that was created in 1883 and is as outdated as an ox-cart on an expressway?

I will tell you why. Because by keeping the status quo, there are votes to be had and soft money to be pocketed. That is the dirty little secret.

When the civil service was established well over a century ago, it had a worthy goal—to create a professional work force that was free of political cronyism.

Back then, it was valid. But too often in government we pass laws to fix the problems of the moment and then we keep those laws on the books for years and years without ever following up to see if they are still needed.

The truth of the matter is that a solution from the 19th century is posing a problem in the 21st, especially when this country is threatened in such a different and sinister way.

Presently, we are operating under a system of governmental gout and personnel paralysis.

Despite its name, our civil service system has nothing to do with civility. It offers little reward for good workers. It provides lots of cover for bad workers.

Hiring a new federal employee can take 5 months—5 months. Firing a bad worker takes more than a year—if it is even allowable—because of the mountains of paper work, hearings, and appeals.

A Federal worker caught drunk on the job can't be fired for 30 days, and then he has the right to insist on endless appeals.

Productivity should be the name of the game. And we lose productivity when bad folks hold onto jobs forever or when jobs go unfilled for months.

It is no wonder there is resentment among out many good employees. I would be resentful, too, if I watched bad workers kept on the payroll and given the same pay raises by managers who are intimidated by the complicated process of firing or even disciplining them.

A few years ago, there was a best selling book entitled, *The Death of Common Sense*, written by a man named Phillip Howard.

I liked it so well and thought it was so on target that I gave all my agency heads a copy and had them read it. Then, I had Mr. Howard come to Georgia and speak to all of them.

Its thesis was that "universal requirements that leave no room for judgment are almost never fair, even when the sole point is to assure fairness," to use his very words. It is still very timely and even more pertinent to the Federal Government than to State government.

President Bush has called his efforts to bring security to our Nation and justice to our enemies a "relentless march."

This Senator is ready to fall into formation with our President's "relentless march."

Because when it comes to protecting the jobs of Federal workers or protecting the lives of American citizens, I know where I stand.

This is a country with 8,500 miles of border; a country that 500 million people enter each year; a country where 16 million containers a year enter our ports from foreign countries, and where more than 1.2 million international flights occur.

The daunting task of securing this country is almost incomprehensible. Let's not make it more difficult by tying this President's hands and the hands of every President who comes after him.

Why are some automatically assuming that the folks who will run this Department will abuse their positions and mistreat Federal employees?

Instead of assuming the worst, why aren't we seeking to create the strongest, most efficient Department we can create?

And don't forget this: Many previous Presidents—beginning with President John F. Kennedy—have found it necessary to exempt agencies from unionization and collective bargaining systems when it was in the interest of national security.

Dozens of Federal agencies are currently not covered by the Federal Labor Management Relations Act: the CIA, the FBI, the Secret Service, the air marshals within the FAA, and the list goes on. And yet the tens of thousands of employees in these agencies have been treated fairly and well.

Today, there are some 800 pages in the Federal Code that already generously guarantee rights, benefits and protections for employees—800 pages worth.

Now, I respect and thank the many good, hard-working Federal employees. And I have tried to imagine myself in these workers' places at this particular time in history.

I am an old believer in that line by that wonderful Georgia songwriter, Joe South, "Before you abuse, criticize or accuse, walk a mile in my shoes."

But perhaps it is because I have worked for $3 a day and was glad to have a job that I find their union bosses' refusal to budge for the greater good of this country so surprising.

Union politics may be important, but it should never take the place of national security. We are at a most serious time in the history of this land. Our country, our people are in mortal danger.

And as I look at what is transpiring around me, this old history teacher cannot help but think about what the timid and indecisive Neville Chamberlain was told by a Member of Parliament as he was being dismissed as the Prime Minister of Great Britain. "You have sat too long for the good that you have done," the Member told him. "You have sat too long for the good that you have done."

I am sorry to say it, but on this question of homeland security, I believe that most Americans think that this Senate has sat too long for the good that we have done.

And as Chamberlain slunk away that historic day, the crowd shouted after him, "Go, go, go."

Then, you remember, Winston Churchill, who had been a voice in the wilderness warning for years about the threat of Hitler, became Prime Minister.

And in that famous speech to Parliament in May of 1940, he uttered those famous words, "I have nothing to offer but blood, tears, toil, and sweat."

Madam President, what does this Senate have to offer? What do we have to offer in this time of crisis? How about a little bipartisanship, perhaps? That is not too much to ask, is it, compared to blood, tears, toil, and sweat?

Because, as Churchill continued in that speech, "We have before us an ordeal of the most grievous kind." We certainly have that today, an ordeal of the most grievous kind.

Churchill went on:

"We have before us many long months of struggle and of suffering. You ask what is our policy?

"I will say: It is to wage war, by sea, land and air with all our might and with all the strength that God can give us; to wage war against a monstrous tyranny, never surpassed in the dark, lamentable catalogue of human crime. That is our policy.

"You ask what is our aim? I can answer in one word—victory—victory at all costs, victory in spite of all terror, however long and hard the road may be; for without victory there is no survival. Without victory, there is no survival."

And then Churchill said this:

"At this time I feel entitled to claim the aid of all, and I say 'Come, then let us go forward together with our united strength.'"

Then, Clement Attlee, the leader of the opposing Labor Party, joined with Churchill as his Deputy Prime Minister and they worked together during the course of the war.

Why can't we have something like that around here now? Is that too much to ask when we are in a death struggle for the soul of mankind?

So, Madam President, I have made my choice. When it comes to choosing between an aged, arthritic civil service system filled with stumbling blocks and booby traps, or an agile agency that is nimble and responsive on the other, this American stands with his President.

I have made my choice. When it comes to choosing between real homeland security that protects somebody's life or homebound insecurity that protects somebody's job, this American stands with his President.

Deep down, I know that I am not the only one on my side of the aisle who feels this way. And I hope that I will not be the only one on my side of the aisle who votes with the President.

Seldom has there been—on any issue—a greater need for united, bipartisan support to make that "relentless march" to bring security to our Nation and justice to our enemies.

[Congressional Record: S8708-8709]

September 25, 2002

Madam President, I rise to speak not on the subject of the war against Iraq—that is for another day—but I rise to speak on the homeland security substitute that Senators Gramm, Thompson, and I, and about 40 other Senators, have sponsored that the President says he supports and will sign.

We do not teach our children the lessons of *Aesop's Fables* as much anymore. The wisdom of *Sesame Street* and the *Cat in the Hat* have taken their place. There is one fable I learned at my mother's knee, sitting around an open fireplace, that I believe is pertinent to this debate on homeland security that has so divided this Senate along party lines.

It goes like this: A certain man had several sons who were always quarreling with one another, and try as he might, he could not get them to live together in harmony. So he was determined to convince them of their folly. Bidding them fetch a bundle of sticks, he invited each in turn to break it across his knee. All tried and all failed.

Then he undid the bundle and handed them the sticks one at a time, which they had no difficulty at all in breaking.

There, my boys, said he. United you will be more than a match for your enemies, but if you quarrel and separate, your weakness will put you at the mercy of all those who attack you.

That is a lesson for today. That is a lesson for the ages. That is a lesson for this Senate and the House, for Democrats and Republicans, for the executive and legislative branches of Government. I am one of the most junior Members of this body. I do not have the experience and I have not seen the number of bills most other Members have, so my historical perspective, admittedly, is limited. But in the short time I have been here, I have never seen such a clear choice as there is on this issue.

For me, there are no shades of gray. It is clear cut. Why, in the name of homeland security, do we want to take the power away from the President that he possessed on 9/11? It is power Jimmy Carter had, power Ronald Reagan had, power the first President Bush had, and power Bill Clinton had. Do we really want to face the voters with that position, that vote written large on our foreheads like a scarlet letter, and even larger on a 36-inch television ad two weeks before the election?

We must give the President the flexibility to respond to terrorism on a moment's notice. He has to be able to shift resources, including personnel, at the blink of an eye. When the Civil Service was created well over a century ago, it had a worthy goal, to create a professional workforce free of cronyism. Back then, it was valid. But all too often in Government, we pass laws to fix the problems of the moment and then we keep those laws on the books for years without ever following up to see if they are still needed.

The truth of the matter is a solution for the 19th century is posing a problem for the 21st century, especially when this country is threatened in such a different and sinister way.

I do not want to belabor the point about how long it takes to hire a person or how long it takes to fire a person. I just know it is too long. I also know that a Federal worker can be caught knee-walking drunk and he cannot be fired for 30 days, and then he has endless appeals. Productivity should be the name of the game, and we lose productivity when we have such a law. That is no way to wage a war.

Do we not realize there is another disaster looming just around the corner, where American lives are going to be lost? And another one after that? And that those attacks against Americans and against our country will occur for the rest of our lives? Would anyone dare suggest that is not going to happen? Would anyone suggest 9/11 was some kind of isolated phenomenon never to happen on American soil again? Surely no one, even the most naive optimist, believes that. Surely no one in this body believes that.

Over 60,000 terrorists worldwide have already been identified. Terrorist cells in some unlikely places, such as Lackawanna, NY, have been discovered. They are all around us, they are everywhere, and when these other attacks come, as certainly they will, do you not think Americans throughout this great land are going to look back at what went on at this time in the Senate? And when they do, do you not think some hard questions and some terrible second-guessing will take place?

I can hear them now. The talk show lines will be clogged, and the blame will be heaped on this body. Why was the Senate so fixated on protecting jobs instead of protecting lives?

The Senate's refusal to grant this President and future Presidents the same power four previous Presidents have had will haunt those who do so, like Marley's ghost haunted Ebenezer Scrooge. They will ask: Why did they put workers' rights above Americans' lives? Why did that 2002 Senate, on the 1-year anniversary of 9/11, with malice and forethought, deliberately weaken the powers of the President in time of war? And then, why did this Senate, in all its vainglory, rear back and deliver the ultimate slap in the face of the President by not even giving him the decency to have an up-or-down vote on his own proposal? This is unworthy of this great body. It is demeaning, ugly, and over the top.

What were they thinking of, they will ask? What could have possessed them? Do not ask then for whom the bell tolls. It will toll for us.

Few leaders have understood the lessons of history as well as Winston Churchill because he was not only a soldier and a politician, but he was also a Nobel Prize-winning historian. Perhaps then at this time we should remember the question Churchill framed to the world when he made that famous Iron Curtain speech at Fulton, MO, at Westminster College in 1946. He first reminded the audience:

"War and tyranny remain the great enemies of mankind."

Then he asked this question:

"Do we not understand what war means to the ordinary person? Can you not grasp its horror?"

Some of the remarks earlier this morning on this floor reminded me of something else about that speech and its aftermath. Churchill, being so blunt, did not go over very well. The American media and others did not want to hear that kind of talk. They called Winston Churchill a warmonger, and even the usually gutsy Harry Truman denied knowing in advance what was in the speech and even suggested that Churchill should not give it.

The old soldier went on and said some other very sensible and thought-provoking things in that speech, like war used to be squalid and glorious, but now war is only squalid.

I want to repeat that line that is at the heart of what I want to say today: Do we not understand what war means to the ordinary person? Can we not grasp its horror? Has scoring points with some labor boss become more important than the safety of our citizens? Can you not grasp its horror?

I wonder if you would feel the same way if the Golden Gate Bridge was brought down and 95 cars plunged into the San Francisco Bay. Could we then not grasp its horror? Would we then in the name of homeland security still want to take powers away from the President?

Or would you feel the same way if that beautiful little city of New Roads, LA, on the False River, with the Spanish moss dangling on those live oaks, were to go up in a mushroom cloud? Could you then not grasp its horror?

We rev up our emotions so easily to fight superhighways from leveling ethnic neighborhoods. So it would seem to me we should be able to get up the same kind of rage when terrorists want to level entire cities such as Baltimore or Atlanta or the manicured mansions of Newport, RI. If those beautiful cities were the target of a terrorist attack, could you then not grasp its horror? Or the Space Needle in Seattle, filled with tourists, crashing to the ground. Or a smallpox epidemic, in days, wiping out completely the Twin Cities of Minnesota or spreading across the forest plains of South Dakota. From the great Atlantic Ocean to the wide Pacific shore, from the Blue Ridge of Tennessee to Beacon Hill in Massachusetts, I guarantee then the country would grasp that war is horror. And as sure as night follows the day, when catastrophes occur, the Senate, us, we will be held accountable if we fail to give the President the tools to do his job.

Why are people back home always ahead of the politicians? Because most politicians, most at our level, do not get out among them anymore. We think we do. And some of us do. A town hall meeting here, a senior center there, a focus group or two, but we don't really. We do not talk to real people anymore. We are too busy in that room dialing up dollars. The only horror we can grasp from that experience is some fat cat telling us that he is already maxed out.

Why are we even in this debate? How will it be recorded in years to come when the historians write their accounts of the days of a Senate in September of 2002? How will our actions be judged by the people who go to the polls this year on November 5? Frankly, I think it will be one of our sorriest chapters, certainly the worst time in my short time here, a chapter where special interests so brazenly trumped national interests.

Herodotus, who lived in Athens in the 4th century B.C., is usually called the father of history. He wrote about the Persian wars, and about the Battle of Marathon, which later historians called the seminal event in the history of freedom. Herodotus wrote that the Persians lost that battle, even though their army was bigger and better equipped, because the Persians committed the sin of hubris; hubris, best defined as outrageous arrogance. If you study the lessons of history, especially the lessons of the history of freedom, you will find that hubris would time and time again bring down many other powerful civilizations.

Hubris, outrageous arrogance, is so prevalent in this debate. The hubris of some labor bosses and their purchased partridges in a pear tree.

Outrageous arrogance. What else can you call it when the interests of the few are put above the welfare of the whole country?

For the rest of our lives, we will have to live with what we do on this issue. Will we choose to protect the special interests or will we choose to protect the lives of Americans? Will we hog-tie the hands of our President or give him the same unfettered flexibility other Presidents have had before him? Do not let this be one of those votes you will look back on and ask yourselves for the rest of your lives, what was I thinking? For as we are reminded in the "Rubaiyat" of Omar Khayyam: "The moving finger writes, and having writ, moves on. All your piety nor wit shall lure it back to cancel half a line, nor all your tears wash out a word of it."

I ask one last time, do we not understand what war means to the ordinary person? Can we not grasp its horror?

[Congressional Record: S9195-9196]

" For those among our troops who are not citizens and who die on the battlefield, I believe the least we can do is to honor them with posthumous citizenship. And I believe it should be done automatically by the Government, with no delay and no burden on the families. ... It is simply a final gesture of thanks and gratitude for the ultimate sacrifice these immigrant soldiers have made for their adopted country. "

WAR CASUALTY
POSTHUMOUS
CITIZENSHIP

April 8, 2003

M r. President, I rise today to share with my colleagues the story of one of my Georgia constituents. It begins with a brave young 3rd Infantry soldier named Diego Rincon.

Diego was a native of Colombia and he came to the United States in 1989 with his family when he was 5 years old. He enjoyed a life of freedom and safety that might not have been possible in Colombia.

Diego was extremely loyal to the country that welcomed him. And after the September 11 attacks, he decided it was time to repay his adopted Nation.

Upon graduation from Salem High School in Conyers, GA, Diego enlisted in the Army. He became a member of the "Rock of the Marne," Fort Stewart's 3rd Infantry Division.

Sadly, Private First Class Rincon was killed March 29 in Iraq by a suicide bomber at a military checkpoint. Diego was 19 years old. Three other members of his 1st Brigade were also killed.

In late February, Diego wrote his final letter home to his mother just as his Brigade was getting ready to move out. Let me read just a little of that letter:

"So I guess the time has finally come for us to see what we are made of, who will crack when the stress level rises and who will be calm all the way through it. Only time will tell.

"I try not to think of what may happen in the future, but I can't stand seeing it in my eyes. There's going to be murders, funerals and tears rolling down everybody's eyes. But the only thing I can say is, keep my head up and try to keep the faith and pray for better days. All this will pass. I believe God has a path for me.

"Whether I make it or not, it's all part of the plan. It can't be changed, only completed."

This 19-year-old was wise beyond his years.

Diego joined the Army for the noblest of reasons. He fought and died in Iraq while defending our Nation's freedom.

And after his death, his family asked one last request of the Government in return for their son's life—to be able to bury him this Thursday as a U.S. citizen.

I am very pleased and proud to announce today that—with the help of the INS—Private First Class Diego Rincon has been awarded U.S. citizenship. This brave soldier will be buried Thursday as a citizen of our great country.

But there are thousands of non-citizens fighting in our military right now.

So, I, along with my fellow senator from Georgia, Senator Chambliss, have introduced legislation calling for citizenship to be granted immediately to any soldier who fights in our armed services and dies in combat.

For those among our troops who are not citizens and who die on the battlefield, I believe the least we can do is to honor them with posthumous citizenship.

And I believe it should be done automatically by the Government, with no delay and no burden on the families.

Under our bill, the families of these brave soldiers would not have to fill out any forms or make any phone calls.

This citizenship would apply only to the deceased soldier and it would not make the soldier's family eligible for any extra benefits or special treatment.

It is simply a final gesture of thanks and gratitude for the ultimate sacrifice these immigrant soldiers have made for their adopted country.

[Congressional Record: S4953]

"A copperhead snake will kill you. It could kill one of my dogs. It could kill one of my grandchildren. It could kill any one of my four great-grandchildren. They play all the time where I found those killers. You know, when I discovered those copperheads, I did not call my wife Shirley for advice, as I usually do on most things. I did not go before the city council. I did not yell for help from my neighbors. I just took a hoe and knocked them in the head and killed them, dead as a doorknob. I guess you could call it unilateral action, a preemptive strike."

SADDAM HUSSEIN AND IRAQ

October 3, 2002

Madam President, I have signed on as an original cosponsor of the Iraq resolution that our President has proposed, and I would like to tell you a story that I believe explains why I think that is the right path to take.

A few weeks ago, we were doing some work on my back porch back home, tearing out a section of old stacked rocks, when all of a sudden I uncovered a nest of copperhead snakes. I am not one to get alarmed at snakes. I know they perform some valuable functions, like eating rats.

When I was a young lad, I kept snakes as pets. I had an indigo snake. I had a bull snake. I had a beautiful colored corn snake, and many others. I must have had a dozen king snakes at one time or another. They make great pets, and you only have to give them a little mouse every 30 days.

I read all the books by Raymond C. Ditmars, who was before most herpetologists of the day—that is a person who is an expert on snakes—and for a while I wanted to be a herpetologist, but the pull of being a big league shortstop out ran that childhood dream.

I reminisce this way to explain that snakes do not scare me like they do most people, and I guess the reason is that I know the difference between those snakes that are harmless and those that can kill you. In fact, I bet I may be the only Senator in this body who can look at the last 3 inches of a snake's tail and tell you whether it is poisonous. I can also tell the sex of a snake, but that is another story.

A copperhead snake will kill you. It could kill one of my dogs. It could kill one of my grandchildren. It could kill any one of my four great-grand-children. They play all the time where I found those killers.

You know, when I discovered those copperheads, I did not call my wife Shirley for advice, as I usually do on most things. I did not go before the city council. I did not yell for help from my neighbors. I just took a hoe and knocked them in the head and killed them, dead as a doorknob.

I guess you could call it unilateral action, a preemptive strike. Perhaps if you had been watching me, you could have even said it was bellicose and reactive. I took their poisonous heads off because they were a threat to me, they were a threat to my home, they were a threat to my family, and all I hold dear. And isn't that what this is all about?

[Congressional Record: S9867]

"It is obvious to me that this country is rapidly dividing itself into two camps— the wimps and the warriors: the ones who want to argue and assess and appease, and the ones who want to carry this fight to our enemies and kill them before they kill us."

TERRORISM AND SUPPORTING OUR TROOPS

March 30, 2004

M r. President, after watching the harsh acrimony generated by the September 11 Commission—which, let me say at the outset, is made up of good and able members—I have come to seriously question this panel's usefulness. I believe it will ultimately play a role in doing great harm to this country, for its unintended consequences, I fear, will be to energize our enemies and demoralize our troops.

After being drowned in a tidal wave of all who didn't do enough before 9/11, I have come to believe that the Commission should issue a report that says: No one did enough. In the past, no one did near enough. And then thank everybody for serving, send them home, and let's get on with the job of protecting this country in the future.

Tragically, these hearings have proved to be a very divisive diversion for this country. Tragically, they have devoured valuable time looking backward instead of looking forward. Can you imagine handling the attack on Pearl Harbor this way? Can you imagine Congress, the media, and the public standing for this kind of political gamesmanship and finger-pointing after that day of infamy in 1941?

Some partisans tried that ploy, but they were soon quieted by the patriots who understood how important it was to get on with the war and take the battle to America's enemies and not dwell on what FDR knew, when. You see, back then the highest priority was to win a war, not to win an election. That is what made them the greatest generation.

I realize that many well-meaning Americans see the hearings as democracy in action. Years ago when I was teaching political science, I probably would have had my class watching it live on television and using that very same phrase with them.

There are also the not-so-well-meaning political operatives who see these hearings as an opportunity to score cheap points. And then there are the media meddlers who see this as great theater that can be played out on the evening news and on endless talk shows for a week or more.

Congressional hearings have long been one of Washington's most entertaining pastimes. Joe McCarthy, Watergate, Iran-Contra—they all kept us glued to the TV and made for conversations around the water coolers or arguments over a beer at the corner pub.

A congressional hearing in Washington, DC is the ultimate aphrodisiac for political groupies and partisan punks. But it is not the groupies, punks, and television-sotted American public that I am worried about. This latter crowd can get excited and divided over just about anything, whether it is some off-key wannabe dreaming of being the American idol, or what brainless bimbo "The Bachelor" or "Average Joe" will choose, or who Donald Trump will fire next week. No, it is the real enemies of America that I am concerned about. These evil killers who right now are gleefully watching the shrill partisan finger-pointing of these hearings and grinning like a mule eating briars.

They see this as a major split within the great Satan, America. They see anger. They see division, instability, bickering, peevishness, and dissension. They see the President of the United States hammered unmercifully. They see all this, and they are greatly encouraged.

We should not be doing anything to encourage our enemies in this battle between good and evil. Yet these hearings, in my opinion, are doing just that.

We are playing with fire. We are playing directly into the hands of our enemy by allowing these hearings to become the great divider they have become.

Dick Clarke's book and its release coinciding with these hearings have done this country a tremendous disservice and some day we will reap its whirlwind.

Long ago, Sir Walter Scott observed that revenge is "the sweetest morsel that ever was cooked in hell."

The vindictive Clarke has now had his revenge, but what kind of hell has he, his CBS publisher, and his axe-to-grind advocates unleashed?

These hearings, coming on the heels of the election the terrorists influenced in Spain, bolster and energize our evil enemies as they have not been energized since 9/11.

Chances are very good that these evil enemies of America will attempt to influence our 2004 election in a similar dramatic way as they did Spain's. And to think that could never be in this country is to stick your head in the sand.

That is why the sooner we stop this endless bickering over the past and join together to prepare for the future, the better off this country will be. There are some things—whether this city believes it or not—that are just more important than political campaigns.

The recent past is so ripe for political second-guessing, "gotcha," and Monday morning quarterbacking. And it is so tempting in an election year. We should not allow ourselves to indulge that temptation. We should put our country first.

Every administration, from Jimmy Carter to George W. Bush, bears some of the blame. Dick Clarke bears a big heap of it, because it was he who was in the catbird's seat to do something about it for more than a decade. Tragically, it was the decade in which we did the least.

We did nothing after terrorists attacked the World Trade Center in 1993, killing six and injuring more than a thousand Americans.

We did nothing in 1996 when 16 U.S. servicemen were killed in the bombing of the Khobar Towers.

When our embassies were attacked in 1998, killing 263 people, our only response was to fire a few missiles on an empty tent.

Is it any wonder that after that decade of weak-willed responses to that murderous terror, our enemies thought we would never fight back?

In the 1990s is when Dick Clarke should have resigned. In the 1990s is when he should have apologized. That is when he should have written his book—that is, if he really had America's best interests at heart.

Now, I know some will say we owe it to the families to get more information about what happened in the past, and I can understand that. But no amount of finger-pointing will bring our victims back.

So now we owe it to the future families and all of America now in jeopardy not to encourage more terrorists, resulting in even more grieving families—perhaps many times over the ones of 9/11.

It is obvious to me that this country is rapidly dividing itself into two camps—the wimps and the warriors: the ones who want to argue and assess and appease, and the ones who want to carry this fight to our enemies and kill them before they kill us. In case you have not figured it out, I proudly belong to the latter.

This is a time like no other time in the history of this country. This country is being crippled with petty partisan politics of the worst possible kind. In time of war, it is not just unpatriotic; it is stupid; it is criminal.

So I pray that all this time, all this energy, all this talk, and all of the attention could be focused on the future instead of the past.

I pray we would stop pointing fingers and assigning blame and wringing our hands about what happened on that day David Acuology has called "the worst day in all our history" more than 2 years ago, and instead, pour all our energy into how we can kill these terrorists before they kill us—again.

Make no mistake about it: They are watching these hearings and they are scheming and smiling about the distraction and the divisiveness that they see in America. And while they might not know who said it years ago in America, they know instinctively that a house divided cannot stand.

There is one other group that we should remember is listening to all of this—our troops.

I was in Iraq in January. One day, when I was meeting with the 1st Armored Division, a unit with a proud history, known as Old Ironsides, we were discussing troop morale, and the commanding general said it was top notch.

I turned to the division's sergeant major, the top enlisted man in the division, a big, burly 6-foot-3, 240 pound African American, and I said: "That's good, but how do you sustain that kind of morale?"

Without hesitation, he narrowed his eyes, and he looked at me and said: "The morale will stay high just as long as these troops know the people back home support us."

Just as long as the people back home support us. What kind of message are these hearings and the outrageously political speeches on the floor of the Senate yesterday sending to the marvelous young Americans in the uniform of our country?

I say: Unite America before it is too late. Put aside these petty partisan differences when it comes to the protection of our people. Argue and argue and argue, debate and debate and debate over all the other things, such as jobs, education, the deficit, and the environment; but please, please do not use the lives of Americans and the security of this country as a cheap-shot political talking point.

[Congressional Record: S3350-3351]

"Why is it there is more indignation over a photo of a prisoner with underwear on his head than over the video of a young American with no head at all? Why is it some in this country still do not get it, that we are at war, a war against terrorists who are plotting to kill us every day, terrorists who will murder Americans at any time, anyplace, any chance they get."

ABU GHRAIB

May 13, 2004

M r. President, here we go again, rushing to give aid and comfort to our enemies—pushing, pulling, shoving, and leaping over one another to assign blame and point the finger at "America the terrible," lining up in long lines at the microphones to offer apologies to those poor, pitiful Iraqi prisoners.

Of course, I do not condone all the things that went on in that prison, but I for one refuse to join in this national act of contrition over it. Those who are wringing their hands and shouting so loudly for heads to roll over this seem to have conveniently overlooked the fact that someone's head has rolled, that of another innocent American brutally murdered by terrorists.

Why is it there is more indignation over a photo of a prisoner with underwear on his head than over the video of a young American with no head at all? Why is it some in this country still do not get it, that we are at war, a war against terrorists who are plotting to kill us every day, terrorists who will murder Americans at any time, anyplace, any chance they get.

Yet here we are, America on its knees in front of our enemy, begging for their forgiveness over the mistreatment of prisoners, showing our enemy and the world once again how easily America can get sidetracked, how easily America can turn against itself.

Yes, a handful of soldiers went too far with their interrogation. Clearly some of them were not properly trained to handle such duty, but the way to deal with this is with swift and sure punishment and immediate and better training.

There also needs to be more careful screening of who it is we put in these kinds of sensitive situations—and no one wants to hear this, and I am reluctant to say it, but there should also be some serious questioning of having male and female soldiers serving side by side in these kinds of military missions. Instead, I worry that the HWA, the "hand wringers of America," will add to their membership and continue to bash our country ad nauseam and, in doing so, hand over more innocent Americans to the enemy on a silver platter.

So I stand with Senator Inhofe of Oklahoma who stated that he is more outraged by the outrage than by the treatment of those prisoners. More outraged by the outrage, that is a good way of putting it. That is exactly how this Senator from Georgia feels.

[Congressional Record: S5459]

“ It has been a long road with many twists and turns, ups and downs, bumps, and, yes, a few wrecks, a road that twice carried me to the highest office of the ninth largest State in this Nation, to all the continents and famous cities of the world and, finally, to the Senate. ”

FAREWELL TO THE SENATE

November 18, 2004

Mr. President, I have listened with a grateful heart to the generous words of my colleagues, the Senator from Kentucky and earlier this morning the Senator from Alabama. I will remember and cherish those words as long as I am on this Earth. I thank each of them for their friendship.

I see my good friend from Montana on the floor. I thank him, a fellow marine, for his friendship.

This means more to me than I have words to express. I did not come to this Senate expecting events to unfold as they have. I guess I am living proof that politics is not an exact science.

In Shakespeare's "Hamlet," his friend Laertes is going off to college and his father Polonius is giving him the usual advise that you give when your sons go off to college. After all the words of caution that I hope fathers still give their sons, Polonius ended with these words:

"This above all: to thine ownself be true,

"And it must follow, as the night the day,

"Thou canst not then be false to any man."

I have always believed that and I have tried to live that.

I have had a most blessed personal life—personal and political. Since 1959, voters in Georgia have been putting me in one office or another, and I am deeply grateful to them.

God has richly blessed my personal life. My wife Shirley has been the perfect partner for over 50 years. She has been my companion, my critic, my crutch. We have two wonderful sons, Murphy and Matthew, and our daughters-in-law and our grandchildren and our great-grandchildren. We are very blessed.

If he had lived, Paul Coverdell would be ending his second 6-year term. As I told some of my colleagues last night, not a day has gone by since I have been here that I have not thought of this good man who left us so suddenly and so tragically.

My most fervent hope during these 4 1/2 years has been that Paul would be pleased with the way I have served and finished out his term. I know Paul is pleased, as I am, that our mutual friend Johnny Isakson, one of the finest public servants I have ever known, will soon be our successor in this great body.

I also wish to say what an honor it has been to serve the last 2 years with my colleague from Georgia, Senator Saxby Chambliss.

Now as this page turns on the final chapter of my career as a public servant, I cannot help but remember how it was in that first chapter of my life. Growing up in a remote Appalachian valley, we lived in a house made of rocks my mother gathered from a nearby creek with only an open fireplace for heat, no indoor plumbing, no car, no phone, and no father.

On summer nights before the TVA dammed up the Hiawassee River and brought electricity to that Appalachian valley, after the Moon had come up over the mountain, the lightning bugs were blinking, while the frogs croaked down at the creek and the katydids sang, every once in a while a whippoor-will's lonesome cry could be heard.

I remember after my mother had finally quit working and was getting us quiet and ready to go to bed, we would play a game. The game would start when the headlights of that rare car would penetrate the darkness, maybe once every half hour or so on that narrow strip of asphalt across a big ditch in front of our house. We would stare at the headlights of the car as it made its way around the steep curves and finally over Brasstown Mountain. We would count and see how long it took from the time it went by our house until its taillights would disappear through that distant gap and was no longer a part of that one and only world I knew.

It was often at this time my mother would laugh and say, "You know what's so great about this place? You can get anywhere in the world from here."

That world has turned many times since I first traveled that narrow road through that gap and out of that valley. It has been a long road with many twists and turns, ups and downs, bumps, and, yes, a few wrecks, a road that twice carried me to the highest office of the ninth largest State in this Nation, to all the continents and famous cities of the world and, finally, to the Senate.

So I leave this Senate, knowing that once again my mother has been proved right. One could get anywhere in the world from that little mountain valley and back again. Everywhere I have ever been really was on my way back home.

I thank all of you. I thank my family. I thank my very special staff who has stayed with me through thick and thin. I thank my friends and especially my God. It has been one heck of a ride.

[Congressional Record: S11448]

Printed in the United States
60252LVS00007B/11